Capital budgeting and company fi

Other Published Work

Business Economics and Statistics
A. J. Merrett and G. Bannock; London, Hutchinson, 1962

New Issues and the London Capital Market
A. J. Merrett; Longman, 1965

Equity Issues and the London Capital Market
A. J. Merrett, M. Howe and G. D. Newbould; Longman, 1967

Executive Remuneration in the UK
A. J. Merrett; Longman, 1967

Private Company Today
A. J. Merrett and M. E. Lehr; Gower Press, 1971

Incentive Payment Systems for Managers
A. J. Merrett; Gower Press, 1968

Housing Finance and Development
An Analysis and Programme for Reform
A. J. Merrett and Allen Sykes; Longman, 1965

The Finance and Analysis of Capital Projects
A. J. Merrett and Allen Sykes; Longman, 1963 and 1973

Inflation, Taxation and Executive Remuneration
A. J. Merrett and D. A. G. Monk; Hallam Press, 1967

Capital budgeting and company finance

A. J. MERRETT

ALLEN SYKES

assisted by P. R. STEVENS

LONGMAN

LONGMAN GROUP LIMITED
London

*Associated companies, branches and representatives
throughout the world*

The authors gratefully acknowledge the help of P. R. Stevens in
revising this edition. P. R. Stevens has kindly agreed to keep the
statistics and tables updated in future editions which will be
issued whenever there is a major change in U.K. corporation tax
and investment incentives.

First published 1966
Third Impression 1971
Second Edition 1973

Library of Congress Catalog Card No. 73–86116
ISBN   0 582 45058 6

*Printed in Great Britain
by J. W. Arrowsmith Ltd. Winterstoke Road, Bristol*

To Huyền – Trân and Dorothy

Contents

Introduction

This book covers the basic techniques of investment appraisal and the related issues in both company finance and corporate taxation. It gives a full explanation of the discounted cash flow method, illustrates its use in some commonly encountered investment problems, and by means of a new extension of the method demonstrates its application to takeovers. Investment appraisal cannot be adequately conducted in isolation from considerations of company finance and taxation. These are therefore examined with particular emphasis on the considerable changes brought about by the introduction of corporation tax. A comprehensive account of the rates of return which companies should look for from different categories of investments under corporation tax conditions is also given.

The book is designed for senior management (financial and non-financial), financial specialists such as accountants and corporate planners, and business schools. It assumes no knowledge of, and in the text makes no use of, mathematics. It does, however, attempt to provide the theoretical understanding essential to sound practice. A number of case studies are given as practical illustrations.

The nature of capital budgeting decisions

An investment decision is essentially a largely irreversible commitment of resources made in the expectation of securing generally uncertain future gains. On this definition investing in short-dated government securities is not an investment decision since the risk is negligible and the investment can be reversed immediately by selling the securities without loss. Investing in plant or buildings, however, is an investment decision because it cannot usually be reversed, that is the capital cannot be recovered without incurring significant losses when the assets are sold or converted to other uses. Moreover, the expected return from the investment is generally subject to a significant degree of risk. The definition of investment decisions also logically includes leasing decisions which commit a company's current and future resources to meeting the lease payments.

The twin characteristics of irreversibility and risk give rise to the critical importance of capital budgeting in the management of a company. With the growing complexity and highly specific character of modern production and marketing methods, investment decisions are becoming more irreversible. Thus investment decisions are increasingly determining the direction and pace of a company's future growth and limit the opportunities open to it in much the same way that the tracks determine the speed and directions open to a locomotive. This and the increasingly capital intensive nature of modern production methods necessitate careful consideration of the methods used for investment appraisal.

The justification for analytical methods

Surveys have shown that most of the methods used in British industry for the appraisal of investment projects are inadequate and seriously misleading. The National Economic Development Council reported that 'Many firms appear to apply criteria for assessing investment projects which have little relevance to the measurement of the expected rate of return to the capital invested. Among such criteria in common use is the payback period, or the number of years taken to recoup the cost of the investment. Even when a rate of return to capital is calculated, the methods used vary widely and are sometimes so arbitrary as to give almost meaningless results. Failure to assess returns after rather than before tax is a frequent and important weakness of many widely-used methods.' (Reference 1.) Although this report was written eight years ago this comment is still largely applicable.

The weaknesses of the commonly used methods are discussed in Chapter 9 and the case against them and in favour of discounting methods of investment appraisal is, in our view, unanswerable. It is not claimed, however, that discounting methods or indeed any other methods are capable of reducing the treatment of the complexities and uncertainties of investment decisions to a mere mechanical routine. The uncertainty inherent in the majority of investment decisions relegates logical analysis and investment technique to a role of supporting and not supplanting judgment and intelligently applied experience. There is ample justification, however, for expending considerable effort in finding and using the analytical methods which best assist decision-taking based on such judgment and experience.

It is commonly argued that the uncertainty inherent in the data on which investment decisions are based makes only rudimentary methods of analysis worthwhile. In short, imperfect data is held to justify imperfect methods. This argument is essentially based on exaggerated and therefore inefficient standards of excellence. To justify itself any method merely has to bring about an improvement in understanding or accuracy which is adequate compensation for the effort and expense it involves. The methods discussed in this book adequately meet this criterion in the great majority of investment decisions and will do so even where the basic data is very uncertain. It is indeed in investment projects which are subject to a high degree of uncertainty that adequate methods of investment appraisal will yield the greatest measure of advantage since it is in precisely these cases that there is often no margin of safety and certainty to allow for further errors introduced by inadequate methods of appraisal.

Investment appraisal under conditions of uncertainty requires the answer to two questions:

(i) What is the profitability resulting from given estimates if they are achieved?

(ii) What is the likelihood of such estimates being achieved?

The contribution of discounting methods is that they give a vastly superior answer to the first question (which should be asked under any conditions) and so enable senior management to concentrate its efforts on the second question which is its main sphere of responsibility. Further, by revealing factors which are critical to the profitability of a project (e.g. selling price, sales volume, capital cost, etc.) these methods enable senior management to fulfil this second function more efficiently by concentrating its attention on the factors which are really critical to the financial success of a project.

It should also be noted that it is rarely the case that a project is subject to total uncertainty. A substantial proportion of the benefits arising from the project, for example the tax savings from capital allowances, is known with considerable certainty, and is not generally contingent on the success of the particular project since allowances can generally be set off against the company's other taxable income. Further, in the case of investment grants—which are independent of a company's tax position—their receipt is a virtual certainty. These highly certain benefits must be taken into account by methods which properly reflect their very considerable value.

Maximum versus acceptable profitability

Improved methods of investment appraisal, however, are also of considerable significance in a larger managerial context. The inadequate methods commonly used hitherto have resulted in a damaging restriction in the flow of information to senior management since these methods are incapable of usefully exploiting data to its fullest extent. As a result, much critically valuable information has been ignored and many mistaken decisions consequently taken. The elimination of this restriction would greatly increase the quantity and quality of information which could usefully be considered in major investment decisions. In particular it would make possible the attainment of *optimal* rather than the merely *acceptable* investment decisions which are characteristic of so much of British industry.

Many investment decisions involve a large number of sub-decisions regarding the type of capital equipment, the timing of the investment, the location, the pricing of products, etc. It is commonly the case that companies are prepared to accept almost any solution to the sub-decisions which will result in *acceptable* returns. However, in their own interests and for the benefit of the economy in general, they should be seeking the type of equipment, the timing, the location, etc., which will *optimise* the returns, that is maximise the real profitability of projects. But such optimisation is not possible with the crude methods of investment appraisal commonly used.

Again, in this larger context it is probable that these inadequate methods of investment appraisal are symptomatic of more important failures of logic, discipline and efficiency. In consequence the adoption of better methods of decision-taking in this area of crucial importance can often reasonably be expected to provide the important incidental benefit of identifying and to some degree overcoming these more fundamental serious weaknesses.

Finally, we would stress that the formal techniques considered in this book are not important *per se*. What is crucially important is that these techniques are used with intelligence and judgment so that they can lead to major improvements in the quality of decision-taking in a vital area of business.

Reading Sequence and References

To appreciate the main points of the book it is suggested that all readers, particularly senior managers other than financial specialists, should first read Chapter 1, Section 1 of Chapter 4, Chapter 5, Chapter 7, and Chapter 9. The remaining chapters are of interest primarily to financial specialists such as accountants or corporate planners.

References are given at the end of chapters. Our more comprehensive book on the subject, *The Finance and Analysis of Capital Projects*, a second edition of which is being published by Longman this year, is used as a detailed major reference throughout the book and for this reason is referred to as Reference A with the accompanying numeral indicating the particular chapter.

LONDON   MARCH 1973

Reference

1. N.E.D.C. *Investment Appraisal*, H.M.S.O. 1965.

Acknowledgements

In producing this book we have had the enthusiastic help of many friends and colleagues. In particular we would like to thank Barbara Lever and Margaret Walton for checking all the calculations, reading the manuscript in draft, and compiling the index and tax tables; and Clive and Tessa Ryder Runton for producing the diagrams, reading several drafts of the manuscript, and suggesting many points of clarification. We owe a special debt of gratitude to our typists, in particular to Margaret Uttley and Jean Lancaster on whom the bulk of the work fell. Finally we would like to thank our wives for their constant support and encouragement.

I

Realistic investment appraisal

The Basis of the DCF

Realistic investment appraisal requires the financial evaluation of many complex factors—for example, the choice of size, type and location of the investment, and the choice of timing. It also requires evaluation of the effects of taxation and different forms of financing. These factors must be taken into account in a manner which is both economically sound and administratively efficient. Only the discounting methods of investment appraisal adequately meet both these requirements. This chapter is devoted to explaining and illustrating the *basic* principles of two such methods—Discounted Cash Flow (DCF) and Net Present Value (NPV) which are described in fuller operational detail in the next two chapters. A third discounting method, the Annual Capital Charge (ACC) method, is described in Chapter 10.

1. The DCF method

a. Defining DCF

All discounting methods require a forecast of the annual net *cash* outlays required to commence an investment, and the annual net of tax *cash* receipts expected from it. Broadly speaking net of tax cash receipts comprise profits less taxes *when paid* plus the depreciation provision. The DCF method treats the net cash receipts as consisting of 'interest' (a rate of return on capital) plus the recovery of the initial capital in exactly the same way as a building society regards mortgage payments as a mixture of interest plus a recovery of capital. The DCF return is thus nothing more than *the true annual rate of return on the capital outstanding in the investment*. Anyone who understands how interest is calculated on a building society loan or a bank overdraft (both of which involve paying interest only on the actual sum outstanding at any time), already understands the principle underlying the DCF method.

In essence, then, the method involves calculating the *net of tax* return earned on the capital outstanding in a project. It must be stressed that the DCF return is net of tax since it is their net of tax income which companies and individuals want to maximise. It is because the DCF method operates on the net of tax cash flows that it takes full account of concessions such as investment grants and accelerated depreciation which cannot be taken into account by conventional methods of investment appraisal.

The meaning of the DCF return is illustrated in the following simple hypothetical example:

Suppose a company invests £200 and receives back £123 at the end of the first year, £123 at the end of the second year, and nothing thereafter. This £123 might comprise, say, £23 net of tax profits plus £100 depreciation. The net of tax DCF return on this project is 15%. Exactly *how* this was ascertained will be considered later (Chapter 2); at this stage we are concerned only with the meaning of this 15%. This is best seen from the breakdown in Table 1.1 of the net cash receipts into the return on the capital ('interest') and the recovery of initial capital.

Table 1.1

Year 1	Repayments Total Sum	£123	
	less	(30)	being 15% 'interest' on the £200 capital outstanding at the beginning of the year,
	leaving	£ 93	capital repayment, which leaves £107 of the capital outstanding at the start of the second year.
Year 2	Repayments Total Sum	£123	
	less	(16)	being 15% 'interest' on the £107 capital outstanding at the beginning of the year,
	leaving	£107	which will exactly repay the capital sum outstanding.

(All figures are given to the nearest whole number.)

The DCF rate of return is thus seen to be the net of tax rate of return earned on the capital as long as the capital is locked up in the project. It seems self-evident that this is the rate of return which is most relevant to assessing the desirability of a capital project. It does not seem either realistic or sensible to try to analyse a project in terms of its rate of return to the initial capital invested (as is usual in the average book rate of return method) in view of the fact that a large part of this capital will have been recovered well before the life of the project is over (typically some capital will be recovered each year).[1] Once capital has been recovered from a project the company can reinvest it to earn its keep elsewhere, hence there is no purpose or justification in requiring that an investment project should go on earning a rate of return on the capital which it is no longer using.

b. The effect of timing

The DCF return arising from a capital project will depend not only on the actual magnitude of the cash flows, but also on the timing of these cash flows. For example, if in the previous illustration the net cash receipts had been £236 in the first year and £10 in the second year then the DCF return would have been 22% instead of 15% although the sum of the cash flows is the same as in the previous example (£236 + £10 = £123 + £123). This at first seems odd but it reflects only the fact that much more capital will have been recovered in the first year so that the cash remaining represents a higher rate of return on the smaller *average* amount of capital locked up in the project over its life. This can be seen in Table 1.2.

Table 1.2

Year 1	Repayments Total Sum	£236	
	less	(44)	being 22% 'interest' on the £200 of capital outstanding at the beginning of the year,
	leaving	£192	capital repayment, which leaves £8 of capital outstanding at the start of the second year.
Year 2	Repayments Total Sum	£10	
	less	(2)	being 22% 'interest' on the £8 of capital outstanding at the beginning of the year,
	leaving	£ 8	which will exactly repay the capital sum outstanding.

[1] The average book rate of return—assuming the more plausible net of tax variant—on this project is only $11\frac{1}{2}$% (£23/200), yet it has been clearly demonstrated that money could have been borrowed at up to 15% and would still have yielded a profit.

Another way of appreciating this point is to consider what higher rate of interest a building society would obtain if borrowers paid all of the payments due over the twenty years on a twenty-year mortgage at the end of the first year: clearly the building society would be getting a vastly higher rate of interest since it would have charged interest at, say, 6% for twenty years and in fact received all this interest for lending for only one year. It is obvious in this case that the real return obtained by the building society is much higher than 6% despite the fact that the sum total of the payments received has not changed. But what is true in this extreme case must also be true to a lesser degree in any other case in which the same total of cash flows is received earlier.

The net cash flow on which the DCF method works is the actual net cash receipts attributable to the investment project after meeting all actual outlays. As stated previously, basically it is the project's profits less taxes when paid, plus the depreciation provisions. Thus the DCF method, as seen from the above examples, automatically allows for full recovery of initial capital, hence there is no need to allow separately for 'depreciation' in the calculation.

It will be seen from this outline of the DCF method that it represents a realistic and rational basis for investment appraisal; realistic because it concentrates on the factual question of the actual amount and timing of the net cash flows. It is not concerned with the legal or accounting concepts of profitability which will typically differ widely from a project's actual net cash generation with which a company must be primarily concerned. It is a rational method of investment appraisal in that it provides in the net of tax return on the capital outstanding, a meaningful control figure for management and a figure which, as will be shown, can be linked to actual returns required for shareholders and allow for all the complex ramifications of modern finance and taxation. Moreover, it is a concept which provides the same meaningful measure of return for all the complex patterns of cash flows including such complications as long gestation periods, teething troubles, investment grants, capital allowances, rising or falling income, etc., some of which arise with the majority of investment projects.

2. Present value and the cost of capital

a. Defining present value

So far we have considered what the DCF return means and how it is calculated. We turn now to a brief discussion of the concept which underlies the DCF method, and indeed all discounting methods, the concept of 'present value'. The first problem of investment appraisal is to reduce to a common basis cash expenditures and receipts which arise at different points of time. This problem is dealt with by finding a meaningful exchange rate between money now and money arising in future periods, that is by finding the *time* value of money.

Money now is clearly worth more than an equal sum in the future. In part this is because of the existence of uncertainty concerning the receipt of the equal sum in the future. It is important to appreciate, however, that a sum today is worth more than an equal sum in the future even under conditions of absolute certainty. This is due to the simple fact that £100 today could be invested and with absolute certainty grow to a larger sum in a year's time. Thus if the £100 were invested in bank deposits at 5% interest it would grow to £105 by the end of the year. If this 5% investment represented an individual's best available use for additional funds *he should logically value £105 in a year's time as worth to him only £100 now. Offered £105 one year hence, he should be prepared to give only £100 for it today.* (What applies to individuals applies equally to companies who, for this purpose, are essentially collections of individual shareholders.)

In this example an investor is exchanging money one year hence for money today at the rate of £1·05 for £1. Thus any sum £X one year hence must be worth only £X/1·05 today. This process by which future money is converted into its equivalent in present money is called discounting and derives its name from the fact that the future money is being reduced (discounted) to its current money equivalent, that is, to its 'present value'.

It is convenient to express the time value of money in terms of an annual rate of interest. Thus if money is held to have a time value of 5% a year, it means that £100 today is equivalent to 1·05 times £100, that is, £105 in a year's time. Similarly, if the same time value of money is applicable in future years then £100 today will be equivalent to 1·05 times £105, that is, $1·05 \times 1·05 \times £100 = £110·25$ in two years' time. This latter sum is simply $1·05^2 \times £100$. By the same logic £100 today is equivalent to $1·05^3 \times £100$ three years hence, and so on for all future years.

Looking at this relationship the other way round, £100 in a year's time is worth £100/1·05 today; £100 in two years' time is worth £100/1·05² today and £100 in ten years' time is worth only £100/1·05¹⁰ today, etc.

Suppose, for example, an investor who can normally invest to get 8% interest per year is offered an investment giving rise to £388 at the end of each of the three following years. The present value of these sums is simply

$$\frac{£388}{1·08} + \frac{£388}{1·08^2} + \frac{£388}{1·08^3} = £359 + £333 + £308 = £1,000.$$

If the investment costs, say, £800 he should clearly accept it since the present value (the equivalent in today's money) of the three lots of £388 is £1,000, thus giving him the equivalent of £1,000 – £800 = £200 now from accepting the investment proposal.

This £1,000 – £800 (capital cost less present value of future cash flows) is the investment's net present value. If cash flows are known with certainty the company can use this net present value as a general investment criterion and accept any investment that gives a positive net present value, that is accept any investment whose future benefits have a current value in excess of the capital outlay required to secure them. This is the basis of the Net Present Value method which is more fully discussed in Chapter 3.

b. The cost of capital

To use either the Net Present Value or DCF method for appraising investments it is necessary to establish a meaningful time value of money to the company or individual concerned. This time value of money is the rate of interest used for discounting by the Net Present Value method. It is also used as a 'cut-off' rate—i.e. the minimum DCF return required on investment.

Determining a meaningful time value of money is considered in detail in Chapter 4. Let it suffice to say here that for a company this time value of money or cut-off rate should be generally set at a level which will give its shareholders the rate of return which they can obtain from comparable investments outside the company. If an investment proposal in the company offers a DCF return equal to or more than this rate then shareholders will gain from the investment which should therefore be accepted. Henceforth we shall generally refer to this rate of return standard or cut-off rate as the 'cost of capital'.

3. Summary

In this chapter we have briefly described the two main discounting methods, DCF and Net Present Value. It is apparent that these two methods are closely interrelated, and this relationship will be considered more fully in later chapters. In the next two chapters we consider each method in operational detail taking into account the effects of taxation, etc.

2

Calculating the DCF return

This chapter defines and illustrates the DCF return more fully than the first chapter, but is primarily devoted to explaining the method of calculation in practicable detail. In particular, it sets out a short-cut method of dealing with taxation, investment grants, and capital allowances. Most of this chapter may be omitted by readers not interested in the detailed arithmetic of determining DCF returns.

1. Defining and analysing an investment, and some basic assumptions

a. Definition

An investment can be defined as the outlay of cash or other resources in the expectation of receiving back larger sums of cash or other benefits in the future. In short it involves sacrificing (or investing) existing resources in the hope of receiving larger benefits later. The main problem of investment appraisal follows quite simply from this defining characteristic: it is the evaluation of uncertain future cash flows to be generated from cash outlays (which may also be at least partly uncertain) made in the immediate and near future.

b. Analysis

The use of the word 'cash' is deliberate because investment appraisal *arithmetic* depends on being able to define outlays and benefits in monetary terms. Investment *decisions*, however, often require the evaluation of intangible sacrifices and benefits as well, but these are matters for judgment rather than calculation.

The use of the word 'uncertain' should also be noted because uncertainty is a very important aspect of practical investment appraisal.

The discussion of this topic, however, is postponed to Chapter 5. In the present chapter we consider only the problem of evaluating sums known with relative certainty. Only when the arithmetic of evaluating certain cash flows has been mastered is it profitable to consider the additional but inescapable condition of uncertainty.

c. The basic example

To aid in the exposition of the DCF method use will be made of the following simple example. Suppose an investment costing £1,000 is expected to produce a net of tax cash flow (called simply 'net cash flows') of £388 at the end of each of the next three years and nothing thereafter. Set out in tabular form it would appear as in Table 2.1.

Table 2.1

Years	0 (Start of Year 1)	1 (End of Year 1)	2 (End of Year 2)	3 (End of Year 3)
Cash flows	− £1,000	+ £388	+ £388	+ £388

It is convenient in discounting arithmetic to assume that cash outlays and receipts occur either at the start of a year or at the end. Where sums of money can more realistically be assumed to arise mid-year, or spread out over the year, simple adaptations are possible and these are discussed and illustrated in section 2 of Chapter 3. For the present we shall use the end year convention.

A final piece of information needed is the 'cost of capital' (considered briefly in section 2 of Chapter 1 and in detail in Chapter 4) which is usually considered net only of corporate tax and which provides the standard, i.e. the cut-off rate, for judging the DCF return offered by any particular project. For this example the net of tax cost of capital is taken as 5%. (This is not meant to be a realistic rate, but it serves for purposes of exposition.)

d. The unchanging cost of capital assumption

It is important to appreciate that in the remainder of this book it is assumed that the cost of capital to a company is not expected to change in future years. Where such an assumption is unrealistic many complications arise and how to recognise and deal with these complications is the subject of section 1b and c of Chapter 12.

2. The DCF method

a. Definition

In the DCF[1] method, as we have seen, the annual cash flow of a project is considered in two parts: the annual net of tax 'interest' element (the annual percentage profit or return) and the capital repayment. The DCF return on a project is thus defined as the annual net of tax profit or return on the capital outstanding (not yet repaid) at the end of each year of the project's life: this return is the true profit over and above the full recovery of capital.

For the basic example set out in Table 2.1 the DCF return will be found to be 8%. That this is the case is demonstrated in Table 2.2 (similar to Table 1.1 of the previous chapter) where it is shown that if a company could finance the whole cost of the project by borrowing at 8% net of tax on bank overdraft terms (i.e. paying interest only on the outstanding balance of the loan), it would exactly break even.

Table 2.2

Years	Opening balance (capital outstanding in project)	Plus interest at 8%	Total debt outstanding year end	Less repayments from net cash flow	Closing balance (capital outstanding in project)
	£	£	£	£	£
1	1,000	+80	1,080	−388	=692
2	692	+55	747	−388	=359
3	359	+29	388	−388	= —

It is seen that the company would exactly break even on an 8% overdraft type loan, and as each £1 of outstanding loan earned 8%, the return earned per unit of capital was 8% in each period that it was outstanding.

Since the cost of capital is only 5% and the project is assumed to be risk free, then the project should be accepted. Where, as in practice, the cash flows are at risk, the prospective return must be weighed against the cost of capital to determine if it is sufficiently high to compensate for the risks involved.

It is important to appreciate the meaning that can be attached to the 8% DCF return on this project. Assuming the net cash flows to be risk free, 8% represents the highest net of tax interest rate at which the

[1] The method goes under a variety of names including internal rate of return, profitability index, compound interest rate of return, actuarial method and investors' return.

company could raise money and not lose thereby, *providing* the company can repay the money as it chooses (which is true of British-type bank overdrafts) or, alternatively, can reinvest the money to earn the same interest rate as the loan. A similar interpretation, which amounts to the same thing, is that the DCF return is the rate of return earned on the capital outstanding in each year. In the example it is seen that the project earns 8% on £1,000 in year 1, 8% on £692 in year 2 (£308 having been repaid at the end of year 1) and 8% on £359 in year 3 (a further £333 having been repaid at the end of year 2).

A final interpretation of the DCF return is that it is the rate of return which discounts the cash income of a project to a present value amount equal to its capital cost. By 'present value' is meant (see section 2 of Chapter 1) the value at the start of the project (at a given time value of money or rate of interest) of the net cash flows promised by the project over its life. In the above example, taking the time value of money as 8% the present value of the three annual sums of £388 is:

$$\frac{£388}{1 \cdot 08} + \frac{£388}{1 \cdot 08^2} + \frac{£388}{1 \cdot 08^3} = £359 + £333 + £308 = £1,000$$

Thus, at the 8% time value of money, the present value of the project is equal to the actual capital cost of the project.

b. Method of calculation

From this last definition and illustration we can see how to go about the actual calculation of the DCF return. It is first necessary to guess what the likely rate of return will be—reasonable accuracy comes quickly with a little practice. This trial rate of return is then used to determine the present value of the project's net cash flows at the start of the project's life when the capital is spent. If this present value is higher than the capital cost then too low a rate of interest has been chosen and the calculations must be repeated with a higher rate. Conversely, if the present value is lower than the capital cost too high a rate of interest has been chosen and the calculations must be repeated with a lower interest rate.

Consider this procedure with the basic example. Suppose we estimate that the true DCF return lies between 5% and 10%. We calculate the present values of the net cash flows at both rates and subtract the initial capital cost of £1,000 to find the *net* present values of the project at these two rates. One way of doing this is as follows:

At 5%

$$\frac{£388}{1·05} + \frac{£388}{1·05^2} + \frac{£388}{1·05^3} - £1,000 = £370 + £352 + £335 - £1,000 = £57$$

At 10%

$$\frac{£388}{1·10} + \frac{£388}{1·10^2} + \frac{£388}{1·10^3} - £1,000 = £352 + £321 + £292 - £1,000 = -£35$$

At the correct DCF rate the calculated net present value is zero, but we have one positive net present value of £57 and one negative net present value of −£35. Hence the correct DCF lies between 5% and 10% and is found by simple interpolation:

net present value at 5%	£57
subtract net present value at 10%	−£35
difference in net present values	£92

Thus, the correct DCF return must lie £57/£92 = ·62 of the way between 5% and 10%, so the return is 8·1% or say 8%.

Tables have been calculated which considerably reduce the computational labour involved in these calculations. One such table is Table A at the end of the book which gives the present value of £1 at the end of any year from one year to fifty years for any rate of interest from 1% to 40%. An extract from this table is shown as Table 2.3.

Table 2.3

Extract from Table A, the present value of £1

Years	5%	6%	Discount factors 7%	8%	9%	10%
1	0·952381	0·943396	0·934579	0·925926	0·917431	0·909091
2	0·907029	0·889996	0·873439	0·857339	0·841680	0·826446
3	0·863838	0·839619	0·816298	0·793832	0·772183	0·751315

Thus, for the 5% column for year 1, £0·952381 is the value of £1/1·05. Similarly, for year 2, £0·907029 is the value of £1/1·05². With the aid of these tables, the rather cumbersome calculations shown above can be performed quickly and easily as in Table 2.4 on page 13. This gives the same positive and negative net present values obtained above and the correct DCF of 8% can again be found by the simple interpolation procedure previously demonstrated.

Table 2.4

Years	Project cash flows (1)	5% Discount factors (2)	Discounted cash flows @ 5% (3) = (1) × (2)	10% Discount factors (4)	Discounted cash flows @ 10% (5) = (1) × (4)
	£		£		£
0	(1,000)	1·000000	(1,000)	1·000000	(1,000)
1	388	0·952381	370	0·909091	352
2	388	0·907029	352	0·826446	321
3	388	0·863838	335	0·751315	292
			£57		− £35

c. The required accuracy of calculations

The discount tables provided at the end of this book are given accurately to six significant figures but such accuracy is not often required. It will be found that for most purposes the first three or four figures will suffice, but the six figures are given for occasions when greater accuracy is required.

Further, in calculating the DCF return we used simple proportional interpolation. Strictly speaking this is not correct as was seen from the previous example. But proportional interpolation gives so nearly the correct result that it is generally not worth the effort involved to be more accurate.

3. Practical calculation

a. Shortcuts with annuity tables

To minimise the amount of year by year discounting, tables have been calculated for the present value of £1 arising at the end of *each year* for a period. A table of this kind, called an annuity table, is given as Table B at the end of the book and an extract is shown as Table 2.5.

Table 2.5

Extract from Table B, the present value of £1 a year

Years	Discount factors					
	5%	6%	7%	8%	9%	10%
1	0·952381	0·943396	0·934579	0·925926	0·917431	0·909091
2	1·85941	1·83339	1·80802	1·78326	1·75911	1·73554
3	2·72325	2·67301	2·62432	2·57710	2·53129	2·48685

Thus, for the 5% column for Year 2, £1·85941 is the present value at 5% of £1 a year arising at the end of years 1 and 2, that is:

$$\frac{£1}{1\cdot05} + \frac{£1}{1\cdot05^2} = £1\cdot85941$$

Similarly, £2·72325 is the present value at 5% for £1 a year arising at the end of each of the next three years.

This table can be used to find the present value at 5% of £388 a year arising at the end of each of the next three years.
It is simply:

$$£388 \times 2\cdot72325 = £1056\cdot6, \text{ say } £1,057.$$

This is the same result as was calculated in column 3 of Table 2.4 making use of the 5% discount factors from Table A.

To find the DCF return of a project with constant net cash flows using Table B, it is merely necessary to divide the capital cost of the project by the annual net cash flow and consult Table B to find the result, usually by interpolation. Therefore in our basic example £1,000/£388 = 2·577 and consulting Table B for 3 years, the result is found to be 8%. (Had this figure not coincided so very closely with the entry in the table, then simple interpolation would have been necessary.)

Table B can also be used to save calculating time whenever a project has even a few years of constant income. For example, suppose it is required to discount at 5% the seven annual cash flows set out in column 1 of Table 2.6. The cash flows are irregular for the first three

Table 2.6

An example of practical discounting

Years	Cash flows (1)	5% Discount factors (2)	(1) × (2) (3)
	£		£
1	600	0·952381	571
2	900	0·907029	816
3	1,500	0·863838	1,296
4	1,000	0·822702	823 ⎫
5	1,000	0·783526	784 ⎬ 3,064
6	1,000	0·746215	746 ⎪
7	1,000	0·710681	711 ⎭
Totals:	7,000		5,747

years, but are then constant at £1,000 a year. The annual cash flows can, of course, be evaluated from the separate Table A annual discount factors, as is done in the table. But the evaluation of the cash flows of the last four years can be performed more easily by using Table B in conjunction with Table A. First calculate the present value of £1,000 a year for four years at 5%. From Table B this is simply:

$$£1,000 \times 3 \cdot 54595 = £3,546$$

This gives the present value of the last four years' income as if it arose at the *beginning* of the fourth year, which is exactly equivalent to arising at the *end* of the third year. Hence to get the present value of this sum at the beginning of the first year, it is merely necessary to multiply it by the third year discount factor from Table A (0·8638) which gives £3,063. This is seen to be only £1 less than the present value calculated in Table 2.6. (If the figures in the calculation had not been rounded the results would have been identical.) Here two calculations have replaced four in Table 2.6 and the greater the number of years with constant net cash flows, the greater the saving of effort by using this short cut.

b. Estimating the trial DCF rate

An even more important use of Table B is to help estimate the trial DCF rate of *all* types of projects, even those with the most irregular patterns of net cash flows. It is merely necessary to take the *average* of the annual net cash flows and to use this average to work out the trial DCF rate as if the project were an annuity. For example, suppose a project has the following net cash flows:

Years	0	1	2	3	4	5
Cash flows	− £1,600	£300	£500	£700	£400	£200

These should be set out in a standard way as in column 1 of Table 2.7 on page 16 and the average taken of the annual cash flows, that is, £2,100/5 = £420. If the project were, in fact, a five year annuity of £420, then its discount factor in the fifth row of Table B would be £1,600/£420 = 3·81. The nearest DCF rate for a five year annuity of 3·81 is 10% (the discount factor for which is 3·79). Hence 10% should be used as the first trial discount rate, and this is done in column 3 where the net present value is found to be £9.

This indicates that the true DCF rate must be slightly higher. An 11% discount rate could be tried, but to be quite safe from having to do a further calculation in the event that the true DCF rate is higher than 11%, it would be preferable to try 12%. The 12% rate is seen to yield a

Table 2.7

Finding the DCF return on a project

Years	Cash flows (1)	10% Discount factors (2)	(1) × (2) (3)	12% Discount factors (4)	(1) × (4) (5)
	£		£		£
0	(1,600)	1·000000	(1,600)	1·000000	(1,600)
1	300	0·909091	273	0·892857	268
2	500	0·826446	413	0·797194	399
3	700	0·751315	526	0·711780	498
4	400	0·683013	273	0·635518	254
5	200	0·620921	124	0·567427	113
Totals:	500		9		(68)

net present value of $-£68$. Thus, by simple interpolation, the true DCF return lies $£9/(£9+£68)$ of the way between 10% and 12%, so the return is

$$10\% + \frac{£9 \times 2\%}{£77} = 10\% + 0·2\% = 10·2\%.$$

With a little practice it will be found that the correct DCF rate can nearly always be found after using only two trial rates.

When the larger net cash flows tend to occur in the first half of a project's life then the trial DCF rate found by the averaging method should be increased as such a project will have a higher DCF than one where the cash flows are spread more evenly. Conversely, when the larger net cash flows occur in the second half of a project's life the trial DCF rate suggested by the averaging method should be lowered.

4. Tax calculation shortcuts

a. Tax and capital allowances

In a large number of cases the calculation of the net cash flows and the DCF return itself is time consuming because of the irregular cash flows produced by investment grants, capital allowances and corporation tax payments. But providing a company has sufficient taxable income to absorb its capital allowances fully at the time they become available (the typical case) considerable simplification is possible.

This is achieved by the use of special tables (such as Table 2.8) which set out the discounted present values of the main categories of investment grants and capital allowances for a selection of discount rates and corporation tax rates. Table 2.8 assumes an *average* future corporation tax rate of 50%, but if the actual or average corporation tax rate expected to be in force is different from 50%, then use can be made of a more general table, Table C at the end of the book. Both tables relate to the following investment grants and capital allowances.

Investment grant

Various British Governments have at some periods given cash grants to certain industries in respect of their capital investments as a means of reducing the effective cost to the industrialist.[1] Currently these grants consist of Regional Development Grants, payable to manufacturing, extractive and construction industries in certain areas of the country in respect of the cost of new plant, machinery and buildings. These grants are for 22% of capital cost in Special Development-ment Areas, 20% in Development Areas, and 20% of buildings only in some other areas. Receipt of grants usually occurs between 6 and 18 months after the expenditure is incurred, and is treated as a non-taxable capital receipt. For the moment these grants are not deducted from gross capital cost for the purposes of calculating tax allowances (see below).

Initial allowance

This is a special allowance permitting an asset to be depreciated for tax purposes by an exceptionally large amount in the first year compared to subsequent years. It is calculated on total capital cost and reduces the amount of future tax-allowable depreciation. At the moment there is a 40% initial allowance on new industrial buildings only.

Annual allowances

These are annual amounts by which an asset may be depreciated for tax purposes. They are calculated on initial capital cost less any initial allowance. The most commonly used method is for an asset to be depreciated each year by a fixed proportion, specified for different types of assets, of its written-down value at the end of the

---

[1] For fuller details of investment incentives and capital allowances, etc., see relevant government publications.

preceding year. This is known as the reducing balance method. In the case of some assets, notably industrial buildings, annual depreciation for tax purposes is permitted only on a straight line basis.

Balancing charges and allowances

When an asset is disposed of by a company at a price below its written-down tax value, then a tax allowance is given in respect of the difference. If the selling price is above the written-down value, however, then a balancing charge is made on the difference, i.e. tax is levied on the 'profit' that arises on the transaction. Where the selling price exceeds the *net* initial cost (initial cost less any investment grant) the balancing charge is restricted to the difference between net initial cost and written-down value.

Given these investment grants and capital allowances it is possible to draw up tables which set out the present values of the grants and allowances for a given rate of corporation tax and different discount rates. This is done in Table 2.8 for a 20% cash grant received one year after cash expenditure, and for three commonly encountered sets of allowances, assuming a 50% corporation tax rate and a delay of eighteen months between earning taxable income and actually paying the tax thereon.

b. Basis of the tax tables

Table 2.8 has been drawn up on the assumption that a company will elect to forgo any balancing allowances due at the end of the asset's life and will simply continue to write the asset down indefinitely. (Companies frequently opt for this alternative to avoid the costs involved in record keeping and making balancing allowance claims.) In other cases where balancing allowances are claimed it will generally be found that using the tax table as an approximation and ignoring the balancing allowance will give a negligible error when the project's life is more than, say, five years.

If the tax savings from capital allowances are taken into account separately, we can then treat the pre-tax cash flows as if they were all subject to tax. With a 50% corporate tax rate and ignoring all delay in tax payments, we could then convert these pre-tax cash flows to their net of tax amount simply by multiplying them by 0·50.

But the typical delay in tax payments is quite substantial and should be taken into account. With a 7% time value of money and a one year delay in the payment of tax, the effective tax rate is reduced to only $0.50/1.07 = 0.4673$, or just under 47%. In this case we could take the delay in tax payments into account simply by multiplying the pre-tax cash flows by $1.0 - 0.4673 = 0.5327$ to convert them to their net of tax amounts.

Similarly, if the delay in tax payments is two years, the effective tax rate is $0.50/1.07^2 = 0.4367$, or 44%. To convert the pre-tax cash flows to their net of tax amount in this case we simply multiply by $1.0 - 0.4367 = 0.5633$.

Table 2.8

Percentage present values of investment grants and tax savings on capital allowances for manufacturing and extractive industries in Development Areas, and net revenue or costs after tax, all for a 50% corporation tax rate, an average delay of eighteen months and an average delay of twelve months before a grant is received

| Rates of discount | Investment grant: G
Capital allowances: R = Initial
s = Annual straight line
d = Annual reducing balance | | | | Effective net of tax factors $1 - \dfrac{0.50}{(1+r)^{1\frac{1}{2}}}$ |
	I G = 20% R = 0 d = 0 s = 0	II (Industrial buildings) G = 0 R = 40% d = 0 s = 4%	III G = 0 R = 100% d = 0 s = 0	IV G = 0 R = 0 d = 25% s = 0	
1%	0·1980	0·4730	0·4926	0·4784	0·5074
2%	0·1961	0·4486	0·4854	0·4584·	0·5146
3%	0·1942	0·4266	0·4783	0·4399	0·5217
4%	0·1923	0·4066	0·4714	0·4227	0·5286
5%	0·1905	0·3885	0·4647	0·4066	0·5353
6%	0·1887	0·3719	0·4582	0·3916	0·5418
7%	0·1869	0·3568	0·4517	0·3776	0·5483
8%	0·1852	0·3429	0·4455	0·3645	0·5545
9%	0·1835	0·3302	0·4394	0·3521	0·5606
10%	0·1818	0·3184	0·4334	0·3405	0·5666
11%	0·1802	0·3075	0·4275	0·3296	0·5725
12%	0·1786	0·2974	0·4218	0·3192	0·5782
13%	0·1770	0·2881	0·4162	0·3094	0·5838
14%	0·1754	0·2794	0·4108	0·3002	0·5892
15%	0·1739	0·2712	0·4054	0·2914	0·5946
16%	0·1724	0·2636	0·4002	0·2831	0·5998
17%	0·1709	0·2565	0·3951	0·2751	0·6049
18%	0·1695	0·2498	0·3901	0·2676	0·6099
19%	0·1681	0·2435	0·3852	0·2604	0·6148
20%	0·1667	0·2375	0·3804	0·2536	0·6196

Table 2.8 (*cont.*)

Rates of discount	I	II (Industrial buildings)	III	IV	Effective net of tax factors $1 - \dfrac{0.50}{(1+r)^{1\frac{1}{2}}}$
	$G = 20\%$ $R = 0$ $d = 0$ $s = 0$	$G = 0$ $R = 40\%$ $d = 0$ $s = 4\%$	$G = 0$ $R = 100\%$ $d = 0$ $s = 0$	$G = 0$ $R = 0$ $d = 25\%$ $s = 0$	
21%	0·1653	0·2319	0·3757	0·2470	0·6243
22%	0·1639	0·2266	0·3710	0·2408	0·6290
23%	0·1626	0·2215	0·3665	0·2348	0·6335
24%	0·1613	0·2167	0·3621	0·2291	0·6379
25%	0·1600	0·2121	0·3578	0·2236	0·6422
26%	0·1587	0·2078	0·3535	0·2184	0·6465
27%	0·1575	0·2036	0·3494	0·2133	0·6506
28%	0·1562	0·1997	0·3453	0·2085	0·6547
29%	0·1550	0·1959	0·3413	0·2038	0·6587
30%	0·1538	0·1923	0·3373	0·1993	0·6627
31%	0·1527	0·1888	0·3335	0·1950	0·6665
32%	0·1515	0·1854	0·3297	0·1909	0·6703
33%	0·1504	0·1822	0·3260	0·1869	0·6740
34%	0·1493	0·1791	0·3223	0·1830	0·6777
35%	0·1481	0·1761	0·3188	0·1793	0·6812
36%	0·1471	0·1733	0·3153	0·1757	0·6847
37%	0·1460	0·1705	0·3118	0·1722	0·6882
38%	0·1449	0·1678	0·3084	0·1689	0·6916
39%	0·1439	0·1652	0·3051	0·1657	0·6949
40%	0·1429	0·1627	0·3018	0·1625	0·6982
41%	0·1418	0·1603	0·2986	0·1595	0·7014
42%	0·1408	0·1579	0·2955	0·1566	0·7045
43%	0·1399	0·1557	0·2924	0·1537	0·7076
44%	0·1389	0·1535	0·2894	0·1510	0·7106
45%	0·1379	0·1513	0·2864	0·1483	0·7136
46%	0·1370	0·1492	0·2834	0·1457	0·7166
47%	0·1361	0·1472	0·2805	0·1432	0·7195
48%	0·1351	0·1452	0·2777	0·1408	0·7223
49%	0·1342	0·1433	0·2749	0·1384	0·7251
50%	0·1333	0·1416	0·2722	0·1361	0·7278

Investment grant: G
Capital allowances: R = Initial
s = Annual straight line
d = Annual reducing balance

It is convenient to have a name for this multiplying factor and henceforth it will be referred to as the 'effective net of tax factor'. For convenience this factor is tabulated for a variety of discount rates and is shown in the right-hand column of Table 2.8. The tabulation is for a 50% tax rate and for a common delay in tax payments, namely $1\frac{1}{2}$ years.

c. Using the tax tables: example

An example will illustrate the usefulness of this sort of table. Suppose a company with a 10% cost of capital is considering investing in a project costing £106,000 which gives rise to an estimated *gross of tax* cash flow of £12,750 for fourteen years, arising end-year on average. The capital cost of the project attracts a 20% investment grant on all of the expenditure, payable after twelve months, and the company can write off against the profits both of this project and of its existing activities 80% of the total cost. The remaining 20% of the cost represents industrial buildings which must be written off at 4% annually after taking a 40% initial allowance. These allowances can also be used by the company as they arise. Tax is paid at a rate of 50% on average 18 months after assessment. The DCF return on this project can be calculated as follows. Trying a 13% rate we calculate:

(i)   The present value of the investment grant for a 13% discount rate is shown in Column I of Table 2.8 to be 0·1770. Applied to the total capital cost of £106,000 this gives a figure of £18,762.

(ii) Similarly, the present value of the 100% allowance on 80% of the capital cost including that for which the grant is received is, from Column III, 0·4162 × 0·8 × £106,000 = £35,294, and that of the buildings allowance, from Column II, is 0·2881 × 0·2 × £106,000 = £6,108.

(iii) The total present value of these grants and allowances is, therefore, £18,762 + £35,294 + £6,108 = £60,164. The net of tax cost of the asset is, therefore, £106,000 − £60,164 = £45,836.

(iv) The net of tax present value of the *gross of tax* cash flow, ignoring the capital allowances which have been separately evaluated, is simply £12,750 multiplied by a fourteen-year 13% annuity factor from Table B, multiplied in turn by the 13% effective net of tax factor from Table 2.8, Column V, of 0·5838; thus £12,750 × 6·30249 × 0·5838 = £46,912.

The net present value of the project is thus seen to be £46,912 − £45,836 = £1,076. The 13% rate is, therefore, too low. Trying 14% we obtain in the same way as above a net capital cost of £46,648 and a present value of the cash flows of £45,089 giving an NPV of $-£1,559$. Interpolating, the DCF return is $13\% + £1,076/£2,635 = 13\cdot4\%$.

d. Shortcuts for other grants, allowances and tax rates

Table 2.8 is for use on certain types of assets in various typical areas, assuming an average corporation tax rate of 50%. For all other cases or for different forecast tax rates, other tables are required. To cover all the useful cases a very large number of tables would be needed if they were to take the form of Table $2\cdot8$. To avoid this difficulty a rather different form of table has been provided: this is Table C at the end of the book. Unlike Table 2.8, in the case of capital allowances Table C shows the present values of the tax savings on such allowances assuming a 100% rate of corporation tax. To find the present value of the tax savings on the allowances for any particular rate of corporation tax, say 42%, it is merely necessary to multiply the 100% factors by 42%. Similarly, the present value of the grants is for 100% grants. To convert to the value of any particular grant, say 40%, it is merely necessary to multiply the 100% grant factors by 40%. All this is explained in the Notes accompanying Table C.

Table C also contains effective net of tax factors for corporation tax rates of 35%, 40%, 45%, 50%, 55% and 60%. The Notes accompanying the table show how effective net of tax factors can be calculated quite simply from Table C for any other rates of corporation tax. Table C is thus of very wide application.

References

1. *Investment Incentives*, Cmnd. 2874, H.M.S.O., January 1966.
2. A. M. ALFRED and J. B. EVANS. *Discounted Cash Flow*, Chapman and Hall, 1966.

3

The net present value method

The most common method of discounting used in business, the DCF method, has been discussed in detail in the previous chapter. This chapter deals with the Net Present Value method (which is largely complementary to the DCF method) and also contains a discussion of some basic practical computational matters which are common to both. The first section of Chapter 11 provides a comparison of the DCF and NPV methods, and sets out some basic points of importance to both methods.

1. The basic principles of the net present value method

The Net Present Value method is the classic economic method of investment appraisal. While it is favoured by a majority of academic economists the method has not found much support elsewhere. In business the DCF method is generally preferred.

a. Definition

The net present value (henceforth NPV) of a project is defined as the present value of the project's net cash flows discounted at the company's cost of capital to the time of the initial capital outlay, minus that initial capital outlay.

Applying this definition to the simple example set out in Table 2.1, and continuing with the assumption of Chapter 2 of a 5% cost of capital for this example, the NPV method can be illustrated as follows:

$$\text{NPV} = \frac{£388}{1\cdot05} + \frac{£388}{1\cdot05^2} + \frac{£388}{1\cdot05^3} - £1{,}000.$$
$$= £370 + £352 + £335 - £1{,}000 = £57.$$

Because this NPV is positive, that is the discounted value of the future net cash flows exceeds the amount of the capital outlay, then the project should be accepted. (Whether this project would be accepted in practice would of course depend on whether the *prospective* NPV would be considered high enough to compensate for the risks involved.)

It is important to be clear on the meaning that can be attached to the NPV of £57 in the above calculations. Continuing for the time being the assumption that the net cash flows are risk free, then £57 represents the immediate increase in the company's wealth which will result from accepting the project. It is equivalent to a capital gain as yet unrealised. It represents the price at which the company should be willing to sell to a third party the right to initiate or exploit the project. Finally, if the company could freely raise capital at 5% interest,[1] it represents the amount the company could raise (in addition to the initial capital outlay of £1,000) to distribute immediately to its shareholders and by the end of the project's life have paid off all the capital raised plus interest on it at 5%. This can be appreciated as follows:

Suppose a company borrows £1,057, spends £1,000 of this on initiating the project and immediately pays the remaining £57 out to its shareholders. The net cash flows are exactly sufficient to pay off the total debt of £1,057 plus interest at 5% on the outstanding balance in three equal annual instalments, as shown in Table 3.1.

Table 3.1

Years	Opening balance	Plus interest at 5%	Total debt outstanding year end	Less repayments from net cash flow	Closing balance
	£	£	£	£	£
1	1,057	+53	1,110	−388	=722
2	722	+36	758	−388	=370
3	370	+18	388	−388	=—

From this discussion of NPV and its meaning it is easy to see the relationship between NPV and the DCF return. The DCF return is the rate of discount which makes the NPV zero.

b. Method of calculation

To calculate the NPV it is merely necessary to discount the cash flows at the company's cost of capital to a present value at the time of the

---

[1] This assumption is, of course, unrealistic but this fact has no bearing on the simple point of interpretation of the NPV method which we are trying to establish here.

initial capital outlay, and subtract the initial capital outlay (as illustrated in the first three columns of Table 2.4 in Chapter 2). It is thus clear that the actual calculation of an NPV is rather easier than that of a DCF return as it involves only one discounting compared with two and occasionally three for a DCF return. Since DCF returns are not very difficult to calculate, however, this advantage of NPV is of little practical importance.

Tables A and B at the end of the book are both useful for calculating NPVs and all the remarks made in Chapter 2 pertaining to the required degree of accuracy, the use of shortcuts, etc., apply equally to calculating NPVs.

2. Practical discounting—some further points

In calculating either DCF returns or NPVs it is useful to know how to cope with two commonly encountered complications mentioned in Chapter 2, capital outlays extending over more than one period, and cash flows arising other than end year. These matters are considered below.

a. Multi-period capital outlays

Suppose a capital project has the following pattern of capital outlays and net cash flows:

Years	0	1	2	3	4	5	6	7	8	9
Cash flows	$-£341$	$-£800$	$-£300$	$£300$	$£300$	$£300$	$£300$	$£300$	$£300$	$£300$

To find the NPV of this project for, say, an 8% capital cost it is merely necessary to discount *all* the cash flows, both positive and negative, to the time of the first capital outlay of $-£341$. The fact that the cash flows for both the first and second years are negative does not affect the standard procedure of calculation. This is set out in Table 3.2 on page 26.

At an 8% discount rate it is seen that the NPV of the project is nil, and hence that the DCF return is 8%. The calculation is thus just the same as demonstrated previously, and it is seen to be quite unaffected by the fact that the capital outlays extend over more than one period

Table 3.2

Years	Cash flows (1)	8% Discount factors (2)	(1) × (2) (3)
	£		£
0	(341)	1·000000	(341) ⎫
1	(800)	0·925926	(741) ⎬ (1,339)
2	(300)	0·857339	(257) ⎭
3-9	300	(0·857339 × 5·20637)*	1,339
Totals:	659		Nil

* This discount factor comprises the present value of a seven year annuity from Table B, multiplied by the present value of £1 for two years from Table A. This shortcut is set out in section 3(a) of Chapter 2.

prior to the commencement of the cash inflows. Further, the interpretations of NPV and DCF given previously still hold. The NPV is seen to be the discounted value of future net cash flows at the time of the initial capital outlay minus not the initial capital outlay (here only a part of the total capital outlay), but minus the *discounted* value of all the capital outlays at the time of the initial capital outlay. Similarly, the DCF return still represents the return earned on the capital outstanding in the project at the end of each year of the project's life, but in this example the amount of capital outstanding is increasing in the early years instead of declining as has been the case in previous examples. In other words each part of the capital outlay can be considered to have been earning 8% from the time it was expended. This can be demonstrated as follows:

Capital outlay at start of year $1 = £341$. With 'interest' at 8% this rises to $£341 × 1·08 = £368$ at the end of year 1. Thus total capital outlay plus 'interest' is $£368 + £800 = £1,168$ at the end of the first year. With 'interest' at 8% this sum rises to $£1,168 × 1·08 = £1,262$ at the end of year 2. Total capital outlay plus 'interest' is thus $£1,262 + £300 = £1,562$ at the end of the second year. If we calculate the present value at the end of year 2 of the seven year annuity of £300 that starts a year later we find it is $£300 × 5·20637 = £1,562$ also, thus proving that each £1 of capital outlay earns 8% a year from the time it is invested until it is recovered.

b. Cash flows arising other than end year

So far we have adopted the convention that all cash flows arise either at the beginning or end of a year. Since the beginning of one year is equivalent to the end of the previous year the convention amounts to assuming that all cash flows arise end year, that is at yearly intervals. What should be done when sums can be expected to arise mid-year, or three-quarters of the way through a year, or spread out over a year?

The first point to appreciate is that where the capital outlays and net cash flows of a project are spread out fairly evenly over the separate years in which they arise, the end year convention is generally an adequate approximation. To illustrate this from the basic example first set out in Table 2.1, suppose the capital outlay of £1,000 is spread out fairly evenly in the first year, and that the three subsequent cash flows of £388 are also spread out fairly evenly over the second, third and fourth years. In such a case it is quite satisfactory to treat all of these cash sums as if they arose as a single sum in the middle of the respective years. The two assumptions may then be compared as follows:

Conventional end year assumption

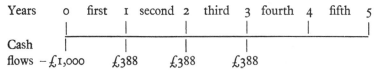

Modified mid-year assumption

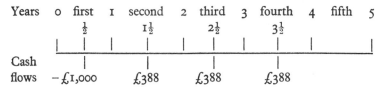

From this representation it is quite clear that the end year convention can be adapted quite easily to handle the case where cash sums arise mid-year on average as there is still a twelve month gap between the *average* net cash flows. Hence the project would be discounted in the normal way bearing in mind that the time to which all sums are discounted would be the *middle* of the first year of the project's life, and not the beginning of that year. In practice it will be found that for the majority of projects it will be possible to utilise this simple adaptation of the end year convention.

Finally, consider the case of a project consisting of an expenditure of £961·5 at the beginning of the first year giving rise to annual net cash flows of £388 spread out fairly evenly over the second, third and fourth years. Because a sum arising fairly evenly during a year can, as has been demonstrated above, be treated as if it all arose mid-year, this series of cash sums can be represented as follows:

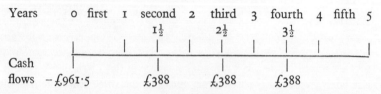

Years	o	first	1	second	2	third	3	fourth	4	fifth	5
				$1\frac{1}{2}$		$2\frac{1}{2}$		$3\frac{1}{2}$			

Cash
flows $-£961·5$ £388   £388   £388

Here, quite inescapably, there is a gap of eighteen months between the single capital outlay and the first positive net cash flow, although thereafter the gap between successive net cash flows is only twelve months. To take this into account the first step is to discount the net cash flows which do arise at yearly intervals. Thus, assuming the net cash flows are to be discounted at 8%, the first step is to find the present value of the net cash flows at the time twelve months prior to the receipt of the first £388, that is halfway through the first year. Using Table B for a three-year 8% annuity, the value of the net cash flows halfway through the first year is simply $£388 \times 2·5771 = £1,000$. The problem now is to discount this sum for half a year only, to the time of the initial capital expenditure of £961·5. If 8% is the discount rate for a whole year, then 4% can be used quite satisfactorily as the discount rate for half a year.

From Table A, the 4% one year discount factor is found to be 0·961538, thus the discounted value of £1,000 is £961·5, which is equal to the initial capital outlay. This makes the NPV of the project nil at 8%, and, of course, implies an 8% DCF return.

To discount for nine months at 8% it would be necessary to use a 6% discount rate: similarly for three month's discounting 2% would be used. (This simple proportionality is only an approximation, but it will be found to be a quite sufficiently accurate approximation for all investment appraisal purposes.)

4

Rates of return standards: the cost of capital

Well considered and well defined minimum rates of return standards against which to judge the acceptability of investments are an essential part of any efficient capital budgeting system. This chapter considers how these rates of return standards should be determined in the light of the 1972 reform of Corporation Tax.

To arrive at appropriate rates of return standards it is first necessary to determine the main financial objective of a company. It is assumed in what follows that this objective is primarily to maximise the return accruing to the equity shareholders. A company may, of course, have other objectives (for example, growth) which are to some degree in conflict with the primary objective, but nevertheless the best interest of the equity shareholders should still serve as a primary point of reference. Moreover, where realistically evaluated, these other objectives frequently prove complementary to that of maximising the shareholders' returns. Thus, since growth can be bought, and generally requires substantial financial resources, high rates of growth are evidently facilitated by high rates of profit.

1. Summary and conclusions

The determination of meaningful rates of return standards is an unavoidably technical subject, which is complicated by its inter dependence with corporate and personal tax rules. The imputation system of taxing corporate profits introduced in 1973 has, however, to some extent simplified the process by comparison with the system of corporation tax previously in operation. It is helpful to summarise the results of the subsequent detailed investigation for the benefit of readers who are content to take the technical justification on trust.

There are three important categories of finance available to companies:

(i)   funds from the issue of shares
(ii) retained earnings
(iii) all forms of fixed interest capital

Table 4.1 shows the importance of these three sources of capital in British industry now. (The last two columns of this table are explained below.)

Table 4.1

Estimated returns required on different sources of capital

Source of capital	Historical proportion of financing*	Estimated rates of return required in future with 4% annual inflation	
		In money terms	In real terms
(i) Ordinary shares	29·1%	11·3%	7·0%
(ii) Retained earnings	44·1%	11·3%	7·0%
(iii) Long and short term debt capital (including preference capital)	26·8%	4·5%	1·0%

* These proportions are for nearly 3,000 large public quoted companies in the U.K. over the period 1954–1969.   Source: *Annual Abstract*.

Consider the estimated returns required in future for these three principal sources of capital, starting with the most straightforward case, fixed interest capital.

a. Estimated return required on fixed interest capital

We estimate that the average gross of tax interest on debt capital will be around 9%. (Preference capital is ignored since it has been declining into insignificance under the impact of the corporation tax system introduced in 1965, and is offered no incentives for re-adoption by the imputation system.) Net of a 50% corporate tax this will cost 4·5% in money terms, or, net of a 3-4% annual inflation, less than 1% in real terms. (If inflation persists at higher

levels it will have to be recovered by interest rates higher than the
9% shown above.)

b. Estimated return on retained earnings

Historically, British shareholders have usually been able to earn
a return net of all taxes of 7% or more in *real* terms on average equity
investments held for ten years or more over most of the last fifty
years excluding the war years. Over the whole period, in particular
since the early 1950s, the British economy has failed to grow at the
rate of 3% or more annually for which it is reasonable to hope in the
future; during most of the last decade the performance of British
equities has tended to fall below the long-term achieved return of 7%.
With the expectations of improved economic conditions both world-
wide and, more particularly, for Britain as a member of the European
Economic Community, and taking into consideration the removal
of the discrimination on dividend distributions by the change in
corporate taxation, we estimate that shareholders can reasonably
expect to receive over the next decade or so a return of 7% in real
terms net of all taxes. This same return of 7% in real terms should
be the target return for the company after paying corporate taxes
and is, therefore, our forecast of the cost of equity capital. With
4% annual inflation this implies a return of just over 11% in money
terms.

Under the imputation tax system the company pays Corporation
Tax on earnings at a rate currently of 50%. If it pays a dividend,
Advance Corporation Tax (A.C.T.) is paid at a rate of three-sevenths
of the distribution, this A.C.T. payment being offset against the cor-
corporation tax assessment on the earnings from which that distribution was made (typically the dividend is paid some time before the
tax assessment on earnings is made), so that the total tax *paid* remains
at 50%. When receiving a dividend the individual is taxed at the basic
rate of personal tax of 30% on the grossed-up—that is, before payment
of Advance Corporation Tax—value of the dividend, but is in turn
able to offset this basic rate liability against the Advance Corporation
Tax payment already made. Additional tax will also be paid or
refunded according to the individual's own tax liability; the basic
rate of tax, however, covers such a wide range of taxpayers that the
average additional tax is negligible, and generally the recipient of the
dividend pays no further tax thereon. Hence, not only is there no

longer a tax burden (as there would be under the corporation tax system) on distributing dividends, but also there is no consequent tax *saving* by retaining the earnings for reinvestment within the company.

c. Estimated return on new equity capital

Basically, as described above, there is no difference in the returns required on retained or distributed earnings. In the case of 'new' equity capital, whether obtained largely from existing shareholders by means of rights issues or—although this is rare for established companies—by non-rights issues to new shareholders, there are the additional costs to be considered of the issue expenses and of the likelihood that the new shares will have to be issued at a discount. For rights issues these have a negligible, although upwards, effect on the derived rate of return, but for new issues, where the discount on the issue price will have more significance, the effective required rate of return is about $8·8\%$ in real terms. Making allowance for an annual inflation rate of 4% this is equivalent to just over 13% (i.e. $(1·088 \times 1·04) - 1 = 13·15$). Higher inflation rates will require higher money returns.

d. Estimated required weighted average return on ordinary shares and fixed interest capital

If a company is to be financed entirely by ordinary shares and debt capital, the company can achieve the objective of getting an $11·3\%$ money terms return for its equity shareholders—whether retaining their earnings or distributing their dividends—and the $4·5\%$ net of tax money terms return required to meet its net of tax interest payments on fixed interest capital, by earning a return equal to the weighted average of the return required on these two types of capital. The weights appropriate to calculating this average are the proportions in which these two types of capital will be used to finance the actual projects under consideration. Suppose a company plans to finance its additional investment requirements over the next few years by a mixture of 80% ordinary shares and 20% debt capital. The correct weighted average would be:

$$(0·8 \times 11·3\%) + (0·2 \times 4·5\%) = 9·94\%, \text{ or say } 10\%$$

This 10% is still in money terms net of corporate tax, so that, in the context of an inflation of 4% annually, the real cost of capital net of corporate tax is $(1\cdot10/1\cdot04) = 1\cdot058$, or $5\cdot8\%$. (It should be noted that the choice of a 4% inflation rate should be appropriate as a long-term forecast but is not necessarily applicable in the short term. Where inflation is at considerably higher rates than this it does distort expected and achieved rates of return, reducing the *real* cost of debt capital and raising the *money* terms return required to provide equity shareholders with a 7% real return after tax.)

e. Estimated required weighted average return on new issues and fixed interest capital

If a company has retained the maximum practical proportion of earnings then any further requirements for *equity* funds must be met by share issues. All investments financed by share issues must earn a minimum return of $13\cdot2\%$ in money terms (assuming 4% annual inflation) net only of corporation tax. The lower return required on any capital partly provided by retained earnings is irrelevant, since if any projects under consideration are shown to be unacceptable the reduction in capital requirements will be made in the relatively expensive new share issue source of equity funds. In short, the *marginal* source of finance in this situation is externally raised equity which therefore represents the standard against which projects must be measured.

In considering what is the true marginal source of finance it is important to appreciate the position of debt capital. The maximum feasible amounts of long term debt capital which a company can raise are typically restricted by lenders to a conventional proportion of a company's net tangible assets[1] for which there must be a minimum earnings cover in relation to loan interest (see reference A 4 and reference 3). Assuming a company has raised the maximum feasible loans on its existing assets and income, further loans can be raised only when an appropriate proportion of new equity finance is provided. Thus, a company in this position will effectively be financing its projects by a mixture of new equity capital and debt capital, and these two sources of finance must therefore be considered jointly. For example, where marginal funds are being raised in the proportion of, say, 80% new equity and 20% new debt capital then the weighted average return for which a company would need to look would be: $(0\cdot8 \times 13\cdot2\%) + (0\cdot2 \times 4\cdot5\%) = 11\cdot5\%$ in money terms.

[1] For a description of these and other accounting terms see Appendix A.

Moreover, a company should regard new share issues as the marginal source of equity funds and calculate the cost of capital accordingly even where it is not planning to raise new share capital for up to, say, five years. This is because any equity capital invested prior to the new share issue will need to be replaced by increasing the size of the planned new issue. Hence the return which should be looked for on the equity financed element of new investment in the intervening years is that for new issues.

Similarly, even where a company is planning to stop raising new external equity very shortly (e.g. the new issue may be to finance the requirements of only the current year) such equity involves a long-term commitment to meet the dividends on this expensive type of capital. Consequently, the rate of return appropriate to new issues should be looked for on any project financed by them. As a general rule if a company is planning to make any equity issue in the next five years or so it should take its equity return standard as the return required on the equity provided by new issues. Where additional debt will also be raised, the required return is the weighted average of these two types of capital.

f. Rates of return standards for normal risk and safe investment

Table 4.2 below sets out the summary results of the previous sections for estimated required rates of return in money terms with 4% annual inflation. Thus the 9·9% return in row (ii) of the first column

Table 4.2

Estimated weighted average required returns in money terms

Financing pattern	Returns required in money terms with 4% annual inflation			
	On normal risk investments		On safe investments	
	Retained earnings	New issues	Retained earnings	New issues
(i) 100% equity	11·3%	13·2%	8·0%	10·0%
(ii) 80% equity and 20% debt	9·9%	11·5%	7·3%	8·9%
(iii) 70% equity and 30% debt	9·3%	10·6%	7·0%	8·4%

is simply the weighted average of 80% retained earnings requiring 11·3% and 20% debt requiring 4·5%, that is:

$$(0·8\% \times 11·3\%) + (0·2\% \times 4·5\%) = 9·9\%.$$

Since the returns in the first two columns of the table are based on our estimates of what quoted companies will earn on average over the next ten years or so they can be taken as the returns to be looked for on investments at the same risk as a share investment in the average quoted company. Higher returns should be sought on higher risk projects and lower returns on lower risk projects.

Another useful rate of return standard is that for virtually risk-free projects. These often arise in lease or buy decisions and some cost saving projects. The cut-off rate appropriate to these cases can be ascertained by considering what rate of return equity shareholders would require on such investment. Given that investors in the company are *equity* shareholders and not investors in fixed interest securities, and given that these safer investments do not offer the high liquidity of fixed interest securities, shareholders must be expected to require a rate appreciably above the expected interest rate on such securities, that is 9% gross, or nearly 6·3% net of tax at the standard rate of 30%. Just how much above 6·3% in money terms (which at 4% annual inflation is only 2·2% in real terms) shareholders would want is a matter of judgment. But given that shareholders have typically achieved equity returns in the peacetime periods of the last forty-five years of 7% plus in *real* terms the acceptable rate can be expected to lie between 2% and 6% in real terms. Our own estimate is 4% but within the range 2% to 6% other views are tenable. A rate of 4% in real terms is, at 4% annual inflation, equivalent to about 8% in money terms.

The above return standards in money terms (assuming a 4% annual inflation) were arrived at by increasing the required returns defined in real terms since the latter returns form the basic benchmark. The purpose of calculating returns in money terms for a specific forecast rate of inflation is for applying to cash flows drawn up in money terms, that is before correcting for inflation.

In some cases, however, it is more convenient to base the calculations on the cash flows expressed in *real* terms. These cash flows should then be the actual money cash flows reduced by the expected decline in the value of money. Thus, if a money cash flow one year hence is £110, then in real terms after allowing for a 4% inflation it is £110/£1·04 =

£105·8, or say £106. It is sometimes the case that the main cash flows[1] can be expected to increase to offset inflation. If, however, this is the case then the estimates can be made up ignoring inflation and the end result will already be in real terms.

Where the cash flows are in real terms it is necessary to set the return standards of Table 4.2 in real terms. For example, on the basis of 4% inflation the 9·9% and 11·5% returns shown in line (ii) of Table 4.2 are equivalent to 5·7% and 7·2% in real terms (i.e. about 4% less in each case).

g. Promulgating a company's cost of capital

It is recommended that as a standard part of its capital budgeting procedure a company should set out at regular intervals its future financing programme (say, over the next five years) and on the basis of the proportions of the various forms of finance in this plan, compute its weighted average cost of capital for the 'normal risk' investment and for the virtually risk-free investment. In the interests of adequate financial control and direction these rates of return standards should then be clearly promulgated to all concerned with capital budgeting proposals and decisions thus providing an essential yardstick for evaluation.

The preceding section sets out our main conclusions and outlines the evidence and logic leading to these conclusions. The following sections consider the evidence and logic in more detail.

2. Achieved and forecast rates of return

a. Historical record

Before turning to the task of forecasting required rates of return in the future it is useful to consider the historical record of the *discounted* rates of return achieved on equity capital in Britain.

Over the most recent and relevant historical period the ratio of average annual net of tax (profits tax plus standard rate income tax) profits to equity capital employed was around 9% for British quoted manufacturing companies for the period 1961–70.[2] This figure, how-

[1] It is rare that all the components of cash flows will increase with inflation. For example, capital allowances are always fixed in money terms, but occasionally the error from ignoring this is negligible.

[2] See Department of Trade and Industry data on U.K. quoted companies in *Economic Trends*.

ever, is subject to all the shortcomings of accounting *ratios* based on mainly historical asset values and profits uncorrected for inflation. A more satisfactory historic measure of the achieved returns on equity capital can be obtained from calculating the *real* discounted rates of return which shareholders, paying tax at the then current standard rates, would have achieved from investing a lump sum over successive ten-year *peacetime* periods since 1919. This is given in Table 4.3 below. (Ten-year periods were chosen as being sufficiently long to minimise the effect of unrepresentative stock market prices over short periods.) Thus the first return shows what a shareholder would have received from investing a lump sum over the period 1919-29. The two elements going into this return are the annual net of tax dividends plus the capital sum realised from selling out at the end of the period. Over 75% of the listed ten year returns exceeded 7% in real terms. No reinvestment of dividends is assumed.

The returns over the whole period 1919-72 are shown at the bottom of the table. It is seen that shareholders would have received a net of tax discounted rate of return in *real* terms of 7·9% from continuous annual investment over the whole period. The general resilience of the rates of return earned by companies is apparent when it is recalled that

Table 4.3

*Achieved net-of-tax discounted rates of return on British equities**

Periods	Return in Real Terms	Periods	Return in Real Terms
	%		%
1919-29	15·1	1949-59	4·2
1920-30	10·9	1950-60	9·7
1921-31	17·2	1951-61	9·2
1922-32	16·5	1952-62	9·6
1923-33	10·9	1953-63	10·7
1924-34	12·0	1954-64	11·3
1925-35	11·9	1955-65	6·2
1926-36	9·6	1956-66	5·9
1927-37	10·6	1957-67	7·1
1928-38	7·0	1958-68	10·7
1929-39	3·6	1959-69	9·1
Average	10·5	1960-70	2·1
		1961-71	0·8
		1962-72	4·0
		Average	5·3
1919-72	7·9		

*For source and method of calculation see references 1 and A3.

this period covered some twenty years of depression followed by a major war and over a decade of price controls under highly inflationary conditions.

b. Forecast

On the basis of this and other evidence it was expected, prior to the change to the imputation system, that, despite the fall in achieved returns after tax and inflation in the later stages of the period under review, the average net of tax real returns—that is, allowing for the falling value of money despite the forecast higher rates of inflation—earned by average companies, (and hence also earned by basic tax rate shareholders) might be expected to recover to the long term trend of 7-8% over the next few years. It is not possible to forecast how this after-tax return will be affected by the change to the tax system with certainty; however, it is likely that the new system will remove the discrimination exercised by the previous system against distributed profits, and, at least while the projected rates for corporate and basic tax are in force, reduce the total tax burden on corporate earnings.

A detailed econometric investigation of American experience (see reference 2) suggests that at least corporate taxation tends to be recovered in price levels. Until further evidence is forthcoming on the performance of British companies, therefore, it is suggested that the net of tax rate of return in real terms that the shareholders can be expected to earn on their investment should be taken as 7% (the lower end of the previously forecast 7-8% range) net of tax in real terms over the next ten years. With long term annual inflation estimated at 4% this corresponds to a return of $7\% \times 4\% = 11.3\%$ in money terms. Inflation in the general price level over the period 1962-72 was 4.9% per annum, but there is the reasonable hope that this rate of inflation will be reduced somewhat over the next decade.

c. Dividend policy and growth

In determining the relationship between rates of return earned on different sources of equity capital by a company we need to use two simple basic rules. The first relates to the impact of retained earnings on the growth of earnings.

Rule 1. Earnings will grow by the proportion of earnings retained multiplied by the net of corporate tax return earned on those retained earnings.

Thus, if a company has earnings this year of £100,000 and retains half of them to reinvest at 10% (net of corporate tax) its earnings next year must be £100,000 plus the £50,000 retentions earning 10%, that is £100,000 + £5,000 = £105,000. Earnings will therefore have grown by 5%. This is precisely the result expected from the rule that the growth rate of earnings is equal to the proportion of earnings retained multiplied by the 10% rate of return, i.e. $\cdot 5 \times \cdot 10 = \cdot 05$.

The second rule relates to the rate of growth of dividends, earnings, and share prices.

Rule 2. If earnings, dividends and consequently share prices are growing at a constant rate then the dividends and ultimate capital gains will give the shareholder a DCF return equal to the first year's dividend yield plus the rate of growth of dividends.

The dividend yield in Rule 2 is the first year's dividends over the initial capital cost of the shares. The following three-year example illustrates this rule. Suppose a share offers a dividend yield in the first year of 4%—that is, the *first* dividend will amount to 4% of the price paid for the shares—and assume that these dividends will grow by 5% per annum. If a shareholder invests £10,000 in these shares then his net cash flows (initial investment, dividends and capital recovery) will be as shown in the Table 4.4.

Table 4.4

Years	0	1	2	3
Cash flow	– £10,000	£400	£420	£441 + £11,576

In this table the £400, £420, and £441 are the successive annual dividends increasing by 5% per annum from their initial value of £400, and the £11,576 is the realised value of the shares at the end of the third year, that is simply £10,000 grown at 5% compound over the three years.

According to Rule 2 that the DCF return to the shareholder is equal to the first year's dividend yield plus the rate of growth of dividends and share prices, this DCF return should be £400/£10,000 + 5% = 9%. That the DCF return is 9% is clear from the fact that

$$\frac{£400}{1\cdot09} + \frac{£420}{1\cdot09^2} + \frac{£441 + £11,576}{1\cdot09^3} - £10,000 = 0$$

This is the DCF return concept described in Chapters 1 and 2 and it is this concept which is used throughout this book when discussing the returns obtained by shareholders.

3. Further considerations

a. Definition of profits

It is important for purposes of the above analysis that profits (earnings) should be realistically defined. Profits as recorded in company reports and accounts are often the subject of arbitrary accounting conventions particularly as regards depreciation. Profits for our purposes are defined as profits net of corporate tax and after providing for historic cost depreciation on a *sinking fund* basis (see section 1 of Chapter 10) where the interest rate is set at the cost of capital as determined by the above analysis.

b. Proportion of profits retained

It is seen from the foregoing discussion that the proportion of profits retained is an important factor in determining the rate of return which a company needs to earn in order to give its shareholders any specific level of return net of all taxes. It must be recognised, however, that a high proportion of retained earnings may have a seriously adverse effect on the price of a company's shares and this will necessitate the company earning a higher level of return to offset this effect.

In a world free of uncertainty it is perhaps true that shareholders would be indifferent to the level of earnings retained provided that they were certain that the earnings were being invested to give them the net of tax return they could obtain elsewhere. In the real world, however, shareholders can never be certain that a company either intends to or can invest retained earnings in this way. Moreover, unless there are special tax considerations (e.g. an exceptionally high proportion of the shareholders are surtax payers hence making retained earnings especially advantageous) shareholders may be justifiably suspicious of companies which retain an exceptionally high proportion of earnings and thus decline to submit to the financial scrutiny and discipline involved in raising external equity.

Hence, the preceding section probably gives a reasonable guide to the relationship between shareholder's returns and company

returns for situations in which a company is retaining, say, 60%
or less of its profits. Where a company retains a substantially higher
percentage of its earnings, a further allowance must be made in the
returns it needs to earn in order to offset these other possibly adverse
influences.

c. Short- and long-term debt

Where a weighted average cost of debt and equity capital is being
calculated to evaluate a cash flow it is important to ensure that the
actual debt used in the weighting is consistent with the cash flows being
evaluated. There are two possible approaches.

(i) All debt capital (both short and long term) can be included in the
     calculation of the weighted average cost of capital. In this case the
     short-term loan inflows or repayments would be ignored in com-
     puting the net cash flows (that is short-term debt capital would
     form part of the capital outlays, and the interest payments and loan
     repayments would not be deducted from the net cash flows).
(ii) Alternatively, short-term debt can be excluded from the weighted
     average cost of capital (which would then consist only of long term
     debt and equity capital). In this case it is necessary to deduct
     from the net cash flows all interest on the short-term debt
     and to take the working capital net of short-term borrowing (see
     Appendix B).

Because current assets vary appreciably from project to project
and because such assets can be financed up to 70% by short-term
debt (compared with 25%–30% as the typical upper limit on fixed
assets) it is generally preferable to adopt the second method.

d. Choosing between the weighted average cost of long-term capital and equity capital alone

In evaluating the net cash flows of a project for which long-term debt
capital will be available, use can be made of the weighted average cost
of long-term debt plus equity capital applied to the appropriate net
cash flows (see c above). This is the procedure which we generally
recommend. It should be appreciated, however, that any project can
also be evaluated using only the equity cost of capital applied just to the
equity net cash flows. In some cases it is preferable to use only this
equity cost of capital approach. This applies to any projects which offer
unusual financial opportunities, such as projects on which exceptionally

large amounts of debt can be raised. Such projects are those involving highly marketable assets—such as offices, standard industrial buildings, etc. (Reference A, Chapter 4, Sections 3 and 4 discusses these points in greater detail.)

In these cases it will often be possible to raise a large amount of debt through mortgage or general debenture finance. To take this into account it is generally necessary to work on the basis of the net cash flows accruing to the equity shareholders, that is to take the capital outlays net of the debt capital but to deduct from the subsequent net cash flows all the interest and debt repayments when such payments fall due. The resulting net cash flows are then entirely attributable to the equity shareholders and the return looked for should be that required on the particular type of equity capital used (e.g. retained earnings or new share issues). Some special allowance may also be required to allow for any additional risk to the equity capital owing to the high proportion of debt finance. An example of this is given in section 4 of Chapter 6.

e. Possibility of external equity investment

If shareholders can invest to get an 11% return this, as we have seen, means that shares will also tend to stand at a price at which future earnings represent an 11% return. But if this is the case then any company could obtain 11%, simply by investing in the equity of other companies. (Under the imputation tax there is generally no additional taxation levied on dividends flowing from one company to another since the receiving company can offset the tax deduction at source against its own obligation to deduct tax from its own dividend payments.) Thus *if a company is prepared to invest in the equity of other companies* it will have a virtually endless supply of investment projects offering a net of corporate tax return of 11%. In this situation a company should never accept any internal investment project which offered less than this 11%—that is, it would never take a lower return merely because of the tax advantages obtained on retained earnings or because of the low cost of debt capital.

While it is perhaps uncommon for companies to be prepared to undertake substantial portfolio investment in the equity of other companies, that this high cut-off rate is the logical consequence of such a policy should be borne in mind when deciding on this aspect of corporate investment policy.

References

General Reference
(A) Chapters 3 and 4.
Special References
1. A. J. MERRETT and ALLEN SYKES. 'Return on equities and fixed interest securities, 1919-1963', *District Bank Review*, December 1963 and June 1966.
2. MARIAN KRZYZANIAK and R. A. MUSGRAVE. *The Shifting of the Corporate Income Tax*, Johns Hopkins, 1963.
3. GORDON DONALDSON. *Corporate Debt Policy*, Harvard Business School, Boston, 1961.

5

The analysis of risk

'All the business of War and, indeed, all the business of life, is to endeavour to find out what you don't know from what you do; that's what I called guessing what was on the other side of the hill.'

Duke of Wellington.

The usefulness of analytical methods in the evaluation of risk has been discussed in the Introduction. In this and the following chapter we shall be concerned with demonstration rather than assertion. This chapter deals specifically with some of the methods and principles. For convenience of exposition, the details of actual examples are given in the next chapter.

I. The critical variables: sensitivity analysis

A simple but fundamental distinction in the appraisal of risk is the distinction between *evaluation* and *calculation*. The acceptability of an investment project will typically involve the evaluation of certain basic data on sales realisations, levels of costs, life of project, etc. This evaluation consists of weighing up the probabilities of different figures actually being achieved. Entirely separate from and different in character from this process of evaluation is the process of *calculating* the return offered if the different possible levels of sales costs, etc., materialise. The common practice of presenting top management with one set of figures and one return inevitably imposes on them the combined tasks of *evaluation* and *calculation* with the result that both functions may be inefficiently performed. The absence of alternative calculations to draw attention to the factors that are crucial to the acceptability of the project may mean that top management's time and energy are wasted considering eventualities which are not important; and their erroneous surmises as to the possible *numerical importance* of particular eventualities may lead to the project being wrongly accepted or rejected. Hence, the first stage in the evaluation of risk is that of sensitivity analysis, determining the critical variables, the sales realisations, costs, lives, etc., which are critical to the acceptability of the project.

An example of such analysis is shown in Table 5.1. The table relates to an Expansion/Replacement investment considered in detail in section 1 of the next chapter and shows the net of tax DCF returns which will result from various combinations of possible capital costs and gross of tax cash flows listed respectively at the head and in the rows of the table. Thus the $11\frac{1}{2}\%$ return results from the capital asset costing £120,000 and having a gross cash flow of only £12,900. If the company is looking for a minimum return of 10% then the critical outcomes are those given in the last row of the table. Given this information management can then concentrate its attention on the likelihood of these capital costs and cash flows falling into the range which will produce these critical outcomes.

Table 5.1

Gross cash flows	Capital cost	
	£100,000	£120,000
£13,500	18%	15%
£12,900	$14\frac{1}{2}\%$	$11\frac{1}{2}\%$
£12,000	$3\frac{1}{2}\%$	1%

If management is convinced that these variables are unlikely to be in this critical range, then the project should automatically be accepted. This situation arises fairly frequently and the project for which it arises may be referred to as a 'fail-safe' project. The first use of sensitivity analysis is to ascertain whether or not a project falls into the 'fail-safe' category.

Detailed sensitivity analysis is generally essential where the basic data is regarded as subject to very considerable uncertainty, or where relatively large amounts of capital are involved; for in these cases management needs to be fully aware of the financial consequences of *all* the likely outcomes.

Where—as will often be the case—there are a large number of significantly different possible outcomes, it will be found useful in economy of presentation to have recourse to graphical presentation. A simplified example of such an application is as follows (a detailed example is given for a major project in the following chapter).

It is proposed to invest £100,000 in a plant to process a chemical by-product and to manufacture a product which has a very uncertain market and in particular, a very uncertain economic life. The basic sales estimates are for sales of between £60,000 and £80,000 p.a. The operating costs, however, depend heavily on the cost of by-product raw materials and these costs could vary over the range £30,000 to £40,000 per annum. Table 5.2 sets out the range of possible outcomes assuming for simplicity straight line tax depreciation and a 50% tax rate.

Table 5.2

Calculation of all possible annual net cash flows—£000's.

Case	Sales revenue (1)	Less operating costs (2)	Gross operating profit (1) – (2) (3)	Less tax depreciation (4)	Taxable profit (3) – (4) (5)	Less 50% tax (6)	Net of tax profits (5) – (6) (7)	Plus tax depreciation (8)	Net cash flow (7) + (8) (9)
1	80	– 30	50	– 10	40	– 20	20	10	30
2	80	– 40	40	– 10	30	– 15	15	10	25
3	60	– 30	30	– 10	20	– 10	10	10	20
4	60	– 40	20	– 10	10	– 5	5	10	15

It is seen from the table that there are four possible annual net cash flows ranging from £15,000 to £30,000 all of which are subject to different possible lives. Calculation of the DCF returns will evidently result in a great complex of figures. They can, however, be represented economically and clearly in the graphical form of Figure 5.1.

The company is seeking an 8% return on capital hence this rate is shown in the figure. This type of analysis enables the decision-takers to see at a glance the critical variables, and hence focuses their attention on these critical outcomes and makes clear the possible range of estimates where agreement or disagreement may exist.

A substantial proportion of projects, however, will not fall into the fail-safe category and the resulting decision at the end of the sensitivity analysis will depend on the *weighting* attached to the favourable outcomes compared with the weighting attached to the unfavourable. Such weighting is clearly inherent in any investment which is not in the fail-safe category. Given this fact it is of considerable importance to determine the best possible decision rules for such a procedure. These weightings are either explicitly or implicitly a form of probability analysis; hence we must now briefly consider what guidance probability analysis can give.

Fig 5·1

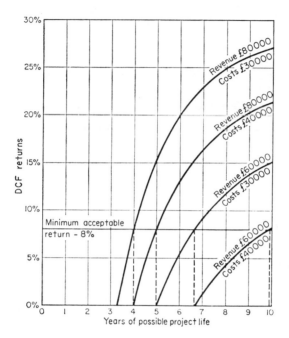

The vertical dotted lines indicate the capital recovery periods,
that is the number of years the project must run before initial
capital is fully recovered and has earned its minimum 8%
net of tax return each year on the capital balance outstanding.

2. Risk, uncertainty and probability

a. Risk and uncertainty

It is important first to clarify what we mean by such terms as risk and
uncertainty. It is commonly argued that *risk* relates to situations of a
type which people or businesses can insure themselves against—as, for
example, risk of fire or theft or mortality. These risks are generally
characterised by the fact that there is a very considerable amount of past
experience on which to base estimates of the probability of their
happening.

In contrast it is argued that *uncertainty* is characterised by precisely
the characteristic involved in that noun, that is, there is very little

certain knowledge. Frequently it is the case that the particular decisions involved—say the launching of a new product or the establishing of a subsidiary in a foreign country—are unique experiences concerning which there are whole areas in which the company has no certain knowledge, for example as regards levels of sales, prices, attitudes of foreign governments, etc. It is our contention, however, that there is in practice no sharp distinction between risk and uncertainty and, indeed, the implications that have been drawn from the sharp distinctions—in particular that probability theory has no useful bearing on business decisions—are generally incorrect.

An insurance company is generally supposed to be exposed to very little likelihood of loss for two reasons. First it is supposed to insure on the basis of extensive knowledge of past similar cases which enable it to draw up scientifically verifiable probabilities of the eventualities insured against. Secondly, they are supposed to insure large numbers of people against identically the same eventualities.

These two factors—scientifically verifiable probabilities and large numbers of identical cases—are often contrasted with business decisions in which the probabilities of various outcomes of an investment decision cannot be scientifically determined and, at the same time, each such decision is unique and certainly not one of a large number of similar cases.

Apart from a narrow field of insurance business, however, the difference as regards the certainty with which probabilities can be estimated is by no means as great as is commonly supposed. For example, if we take the problem of estimating the probability of individuals in a given age and health group dying by a certain age, it is certainly true that there is a great deal of past statistical information on similar age and health groups. But the difficulty is that new factors, such as improved diet and advances in modern medicines, are continually arising and tending to make past data obsolete. The rate of improvement in medical science is, of course, unpredictable and a single major advance as, for example, the cure of a major disease, could significantly alter the average expectation of life. Probabilities based on past experience, therefore, have to be 'adjusted' to allow for the trend of improvement in life expectancy. But this trend adjustment is based on little more than the extrapolation of past experience which is involved in many of the sales forecasts which enter into business decisions. Albeit in a generally simpler context the insurance company is engaged in precisely the activity described in the opening quotation from the Duke of Wellington

—endeavouring to find out what it does not know from what it does. This, we would suggest, is precisely the activity in which companies are engaged when endeavouring to take rational decisions under conditions of uncertainty.

b. The relevance of large numbers

It is sometimes argued that probability theory is no guide to rational decision taking in business because, even where the probabilities of the various outcomes associated with a particular investment decision could be accurately estimated, the company has only one trial of this particular game of chance and the theory of probability is only a useful guide where a large number of trials of the same game of chance are involved. Suppose, for example, the investment decision is akin to betting on the throw of a coin with heads resulting in a profit of £2 million and tails resulting in a loss of £1 million. Since either of these two eventualities is equally probable the expected profit in this case is 0·5 × £2 million − 0·5 × £1 million = £500,000. This is certainly the outcome we should expect on *average* if we invested in twenty or thirty investment projects of this kind. But does it make any sense to decide in one single case by what would happen on average for a very large number of cases ?

It would indeed be misleading to act on this basis if the investment in question was the only investment of any kind which the company proposed to undertake over the next few years. But where the investment is, as would typically be the case, merely one of a very large number of *different* and *independent* investments which the company is undertaking in this and in future years, basing decisions on the expected value of profit—that is what would be expected from a large number of identical investments—is still generally the best course of action. For it is a basic law of probability that a large number of trials *even of totally different* games of chance will result in an actual profit which is equal to the sum of the *average* profits which would have been expected from large numbers of trials of each game of chance separately. Thus, in the simple case considered above it is to be expected that on average the company would obtain £500,000 from each such investment. On exactly the same basis the company might expect to obtain £2 million from another quite different and independent investment, £3 million from yet another different and independent investment, etc. Providing (a) that there are a large number of such *different* and *independent* investments, and (b) that the probabilities in each case are calculated correctly, the company will obtain an actual total profit which is equal to £500,000 plus £2 million plus £3 million, etc. The *individual* investment may show profits very wide of their expected value, but the actual *total profit* from all the investments will nevertheless equal the *total expected* profit. This phenomenon is in fact commonly encountered in business—as for example where *total* cost estimates, prove approximately correct while their component estimates prove to be wildly incorrect.

The important qualifications here are that the probabilities are accurately estimated in the first place and that the investments are really independent of each other. If, for example, a company invested in several different places in the country to produce identically the same product, then these investments are not really independent—if the particular product becomes obsolete, the profitability of all of these investments would be affected. Hence in this case the law just stated would not operate.

3. Allowing for risk

a. Method of approach

The conclusion from the previous section is that analysis must be based either implicitly or explicitly on estimating the probabilities of the various outcomes involved in the investment decision, and that the estimation of these probabilities needs to be based on the Wellingtonian process of past experience modified to take account of new and different factors in the current situation. We do not wish in any way to attempt to minimise the difficulties and the errors inevitably involved in this process; but given that this procedure is inescapable in any rational approach to investment decision no other course of action can be relevant and therefore worth attempting at all.

b. Most probable and expected outcome

A simple but most important distinction to which the probability approach leads us is the distinction between the *most probable* outcome and the *expected* (or average) outcome and the critical necessity to focus the business decision on the latter *not the former*. The distinction between these two terms is illustrated in Table 5.3 on page 51.

The table relates to a simple hypothetical example in which it is

Table 5.3

Possible reaction of competitors	Probability	Profits (£'000's)	Weighted Profits (£000's)
A. Do nothing	0·10	130	13
B. Reduce prices moderately	0·50	100	50
C. Introduce a new product	0·40	20	8
	Expected 'average' outcome:		71

supposed that a company is considering the introduction of a new product and trying to assess the actual profits it might obtain given the different competitive conditions A, B and C. The most favourable outcome A is that competitors will simply continue as at present; the least favourable outcome C is that competitors will introduce a comparable new product of their own which they are rumoured to be developing.

The assessment of the forecaster is nevertheless that the most probable outcome is B (which leads to £100,000 of profits) to which he assigns a probability of 0·5—that is, it has a 50% chance of occurring. But the expected—the weighted average—outcome is only £71,000. This figure is clearly what would result on average from a large number of investments identical to those considered in the table. From the analysis given in section 1 it is clear that it is basically on this average outcome that the decision to invest must be taken. Although the most probable outcome is frequently confused with the expected or average outcome, it is essentially *irrelevant* to the investment decision save as a factor to be taken into account in computing or evaluating this expected outcome.

Moreover, this type of situation in which the expected outcome is appreciably less than the most probable outcome is of very frequent occurrence in business. For it is typically the case that if a particular investment proves successful other companies will attempt to imitate it or to take countermeasures which will give the more profitable outcomes a low probability. On the other hand, if the product proves a failure it will not be the case that other companies will hasten to share the unprofitability of this investment. In other words, competition makes for an asymmetry of investment risks.

In computing the expected outcome it will generally only prove worth while to consider three outcomes; first, the most probable; second, the weighted average of the outcomes which are *more favourable* than the most probable; and third, the weighted average of the outcomes which are *less favourable* than the most probable. An example of this procedure is shown in Chapter 6, section 1.

c. Confidence levels

In any efficient system of capital budgeting and financial control the key factor is clarity of concept and statement. The important distinction between the most probable and the expected outcome has already been referred to. It is also important to avoid nebulous descriptions of estimates as 'most pessimistic' or 'most optimistic'. Literally the most pessimistic must generally mean total annihilation and the most optimistic could mean almost anything. The most efficient procedure will generally be for a company to establish specific rates of return requirements normally expected from investments and require that the proposers of projects provide an estimate of the probability of this minimum return being achieved or exceeded.

It is then possible for a company to set up specific standards and thus impose a systematic and specific policy towards risk. Thus, if a company considers itself at present exposed to a high degree of risk, it may establish the requirement that all projects must be considered by the initiators as having at least a 60% chance of achieving or exceeding the company's minimum rate of return standard. Again, if a company is already heavily committed to a particular line of business so that additional investment will depend on the same risks as existing investments (that is, the successive investments are not really independent in terms of risk) then it may wish to insist that any further investment in this particular branch of the business must be estimated to have at least an 80% chance of achieving or exceeding the company's minimum rate of return standard.

4. The problem of total uncertainty

The preceding analysis has been based on the assumption that it was possible to attach worthwhile (i.e. non-arbitrary) probabilities to various outcomes. We must now briefly consider the possible criteria (developed by modern decision theory—see reference 1) which might be used under conditions of total uncertainty in which no worthwhile probabilities can be arrived at. The criteria are best considered in the context of a specific hypothetical example. Suppose a company is evaluating several possible sizes of plant to supply a new product. The larger plants show considerable economies of scale in construction, compared with expansion of initially smaller plants at a later date. The possible rates of growth of the market are 0%, 5% and 10% per annum. Depending on these rates of growth the company might make the profits set out in Table 5.4.

Table 5.4

Size of plant	Growth rate		
	0%	5%	10%
Small	£100,000	£120,000	£140,000
Medium	£90,000	£190,000	£200,000
Large	£80,000	£110,000	£230,000

Assuming the table represents all the outcomes thought reasonably possible and that there is insufficient information to say which rate of growth is the most probable, what criterion could the company use to make the choice? The answer to this question is, it must be stressed, a matter of value judgments: the only role of logic in this decision is to ensure that the value judgments are consistent and the choice is made on a logical development of these judgments.

a. Criterion of pessimism (minimax criterion)

One such value judgment might be to take the plant size which is the best if in each case we assume that the actual rate of growth that occurs will be the worst possible for the size of plant actually chosen. This criterion would lead to the acceptance of the small-size plant since its worst possible outcome of £100,000 is better than the worst outcome of the medium size plant (£90,000) or the worst outcome for the large size plant (£80,000).

b. Criterion of equal probabilities (the Laplace criterion)

An alternative criterion—which has at least the merit of considerable antiquity—is that of assuming all the eventualities are equally probable. Thus if the company establishes a small plant there are three possible outcomes namely, profits of £100,000, £120,000 and £140,000, depending on the three possible rates of growth. If they each have an equal $(33\frac{1}{3}\%)$ chance of occurring, it could take the average or expected value of the profits resulting from this size of plant as $\frac{1}{3} \times £100,000 + \frac{1}{3} \times £120,000 + \frac{1}{3} \times £140,000 = £120,000$. On the same basis the medium sized plant would have an expected profit of $\frac{1}{3} \times £90,000 + \frac{1}{3} \times £190,000 + \frac{1}{3} \times £200,000 = £160,000$ and the large size $\frac{1}{3} \times £80,000 + \frac{1}{3} \times £110,000 + \frac{1}{3} \times £230,000 = £140,000$. On this criterion the company should therefore select the medium-sized plant with the expected profit of £160,000.

c. Conclusion

It has only been possible to outline the nature of two possible criteria proposed for conditions of total uncertainty but further analysis and references will be found in reference 1. In the majority of business decisions the criteria used will generally be far more complex than those outlined above and, moreover, will probably vary between the different members of the top management team involved in the decision. Thus the criterion of pessimism would rarely be followed rigorously. In the example quoted above, many would want to argue for the large plant on the grounds that, on the worst assumptions (the 0% growth rate), it would show a profit of only £20,000 less than the small plant but offered the possibility of making £230,000 – £140,000 = £90,000 more profit than the small plant if the 10% growth rate materialised.

It is also relatively rare for there to be *total* uncertainty and hence the typical problem is that of modifying the probability approach to allow for this uncertainty. Setting out the general and precise procedure by which this is achieved by the changing group of individuals who are required to take investment decisions, does not seem possible in the present state of knowledge. If the data is adequately presented, however, it is nevertheless possible to facilitate this complex process of sound decision-taking. The illustration of this forms the subject of our next chapter.

Reference

1. DAVID W. MILLER and MARTIN K. STARR, *Executive Decisions and Operations Research*, Prentice-Hall, 1960, Chapters 4 and 5.

6

Three case studies

In this chapter we consider three basic case studies. These comprise a replacement expansion problem, a lease or buy problem and a major new project. These examples are chosen to illustrate basic principles, in particular risk, incremental analysis, and the layout of the basic capital budgeting forms. The major project also illustrates the analysis and presentation of complex financial information for negotiating purposes.

I. Replacement expansion

a. Basic data

This example is designed to illustrate certain aspects of replacement decisions and the analysis of risk.

A company undertakes a large amount of short-term contract milling operations but its existing large-scale labour intensive milling facilities have reached the stage at which it is impractical to continue them in further use owing to maintenance difficulties and manpower shortages. The investment proposal is for the company to replace these old milling facilities by a new large capacity Plano Mill with an estimated installed cost of £100,000 and an estimated life of fourteen years. The displaced milling facilities will be retained for stand-by purposes and for occasional use on specific jobs. Their value in these functions is not numerically important.

The most probable outcome as regards profitability on the new mill is that it will produce about £12,900 of additional earnings a year—representing savings on existing work of about £7,900, and £5,000 of new business. There is some chance that it will be possible to secure rather more new business; but there is a significant chance that the existing business, which is some two-thirds on behalf of a single customer, would decline away over the years as the particular component on which the milling facilities are used is displaced by structures which require no milling.

On either side of the most probable outcome there is, therefore, a whole range of different outcomes. But to all worthwhile accuracy these are summarised as in Table 6.1.

Table 6.1

Outcome	Probability (1)	Gross cash flow first year (2)	Growth of cash flow (3)	Weighted first year gross cash flow = (1) × (2)	Weighted growth of cash flow = (1) × (3)
		£	£	£	£
Better	·2	13,500	+ 500p.a.	2,700	+ 100
Most probable	·5	12,900	0	6,450	0
Worse	·3	12,000	− 1000p.a.	3,600	− 300
Weighted average				12,750	− 200

In this table the whole range of outcomes better than the 'most probable' is represented as having a weighting—a probability—of ·2 and an average outcome of gross of tax cash flows equal to £13,500 per annum, increasing by about £500 per annum. Multiplying each possible outcome by its probability we arrive at the figures in the final column and the average outcome (the weighted average outcome) as £12,750 declining by £200. If there were a large number of investments of precisely this type, then this is the *average* series of gross cash flows we should expect to obtain.

In a similar way we need to allow for the average outcome as regards the capital cost of the new mill. In this case the company is unable to obtain a fixed price quotation and the table of outcomes is that shown in Table 6.2.

Table 6.2

	Weighted average capital cost		
Outcome	Probability (1)	Capital cost (2)	Weighted capital cost (3) = (1) × (2)
Better	Zero	—	—
Most probable	·7	£100,000	£70,000
Worse	·3	£120,000	£36,000
	Weighted average		£106,000

The weighted average outcome in this case is seen to be £106,000, hence the weighted average outcome to be shown on the investment appraisal form will be that related to a capital cost of £106,000 and an annual gross cash flow of £12,750 declining by £200 a year.

The constant decline in the cash flows in this case makes it necessary to undertake year-by-year discounting over the fourteen years. This calculation is relatively simple, but too long for convenient illustration here; the reader will find that, net of a corporate tax of 50%, the DCF return will be 12%. This is then the expected or average return on which the main evaluation of the project should be based.

b. Sensitivity analysis and confidence levels

In this example the project is somewhat marginal if the company is looking for a return of 11% and it is desirable to set out the main outcomes and ascertain the returns offered. This is given in Table 6.3 and has already been commented on in Chapter 5, section 1.

Table 6.3

Gross cash flows		Capital cost			
		£100,000 (·7)		£120,000 (·3)	
£13,500	(·2)	(·14)	18%	(·06)	15%
£12,900	(·5)	(·35)	$14\frac{1}{2}$%	(·15)	$11\frac{1}{2}$%
£12,000	(·3)	(·21)	$3\frac{1}{2}$%	(·09)	1%

It may also be useful to work out the probability of the company's minimum required rate of return being achieved or exceeded. This calculation is as follows. The bracketed figures in the table are the probabilities—thus the (·7) after the £100,000 is the probability of the capital cost being £100,000. It is expected that 20% of the cases in which the capital cost is £100,000 will occur in conjunction with the gross cash flow being £13,500 because, as is shown in the table, in 20% of all the outcomes we would expect the gross of tax cash flow to be £13,500. Hence, the proportion of the outcomes in which the capital cost is £100,000 and the gross cash flow is £13,500 will be ·2 × ·7 = ·14. This ·14 is then the probability of these two separate eventualities occurring together and this is the origin of the (·14) shown in the first row and first column of the table.

This combination of outcomes consisting of a gross cash flow of £13,500 growing by £500 per annum, and a capital cost of £100,000,

would give a DCF return of 18% (as can be ascertained from calculation).

All the other entries in the table are computed in precisely the same
way. Thus, in 30% of the cases we would expect the capital cost to be
£120,000 and would also expect 50% of this 30% to be combined with
a gross cash flow of £12,900. Hence, the probability of these two events
both occurring is $\cdot3 \times \cdot5 = \cdot15$, as shown in the last column and second
row of the table with an $11\frac{1}{2}$% return.

Of the six possibilities set out in the table four will give a return of
11% or more. These are the 18%, $14\frac{1}{2}$%, 15%, and $11\frac{1}{2}$%. These are
seen to have combined probabilities of $\cdot14 + \cdot35 + \cdot06 + \cdot15 = \cdot70$. In
other words, in 70% of the cases we would expect the outcome to be
more than 10% and this is the origin of the 70% in the appraisal form
on page 59. This can be considered the confidence level of the project.

This analysis therefore indicates that although the return of 12%
seems rather marginal the project has a high probability (70%) of
achieving the minimum 11% rate of return and (subject, of course, to
top management's confidence in the underlying probabilities) this
project should be accepted.

As an illustration of the possible layout which the company may like
to see, the basic data and results are shown on the Standard Investment
Appraisal Form on page 59. The extent of analysis undertaken and
shown on the final appraisal form cannot, of course, be rigidly laid
down since it will vary from project to project. Other projects may
warrant a greater or lesser degree of analysis.

2. Incremental analysis: alternative lease terms

a. Basic data

The following example illustrates the basic logic of the *incremental* cash
flow approach and the method of dealing with capital outlays over more
than one period in relation to one of the commonest types of capital
projects encountered, choosing among various leasing possibilities. In
the subsequent section the best of the leasing possibilities is compared with outright purchase.

A company has decided to acquire a computer which is expected to
have a five year life with a negligible residual value. It has to choose
between the means of acquisition set out in Table 6.4 on page 60.

CAPITAL BUDGETING STANDARD FORM

BUDGET ITEM SUMMARY Function	Company Name Location
Budget Item No. I	

TITLE Plano Mill	BUDGET AMOUNT
BUDGET CLASSIFICATION Manufacturing CORPORATE EFFECT Replacement/Exp.	£106,000

DESCRIPTION

Technical Data

BASIS FOR ECONOMIC CALCULATION

Average return based on gross savings of £12,750 (declining to £10,150 over the project's 14-year life) and capital cost of £106,000. Most probable return based on gross earnings of £12,900 (£7,900 from existing business and £5,000 new business) and capital cost £100,000

CASH FLOW PROFILE SUMMARY

Budget amount	£106,000	DCF—Average return 12%
Associated facilities	–	DCF—Most probable
Future capital	–	return $14\frac{1}{2}$%
Investment	–	Year of:
Inventories	–	Initial outlay 19XX
Non-recurring expense	–	Startup of
Investment credits	(–)	operations 19XX
Other	–	
Total of above items	£106,000	

EFFECT ON ECONOMICS OF CHANGES IN MAJOR FACTORS

$\pm$£10,000 on Capital Cost: $\pm 1\frac{1}{2}$% on return

$\pm$£1,000 on Earnings: $\pm 1\frac{1}{2}$% on return

JUSTIFICATION

With maintenance and manning problems on the existing obsolete milling facilities it is essential either to terminate these operations when existing contracts expire next year or to undertake this major expansion/replacement investment. The return of 12% is relatively low but it is estimated that the chance of our achieving 11% minimum standard or better is about 70%

Date prepared: X/Y/Z   Expenditures in 19MM   19MN

Table 6.4

Schemes		Capital cost	Annual cost before tax
I	Outright purchase	£88,400	Nil
2	Main rental payments* over three years	Nil	£30,958 for three years; £884 for next two years
3	Main rental payments* over four years	Nil	£24,504 for four years; £884 for fifth year
4	Rental payments* over five years	Nil	£20,951 for five years

* All rental payments are quarterly in advance.

All four possible means of acquisition involve exactly the same level of service and the cost of this is included in the sums set out. The first step in the analysis is to establish the best choice amongst the three leasing schemes. This is done on the basis of the *incremental cash flows* comparing first the scheme which has the lowest first year cost (Scheme 4) with the scheme which has the second lowest cost (Scheme 3).

b. Comparison of leasing schemes

A comparison of Schemes 3 and 4 is given in Table 6.5.

Table 6.5

Comparison of schemes 3 and 4

Schemes	Years 1	2	3	4	5
	£	£	£	£	£
4	20,951	20,951	20,951	20,951	20,951
3	24,504	24,504	24,504	24,504	884
Incremental cash flows (before tax)	−3,553	−3,553	−3,553	−3,553	20,067

In this comparison we simply subtract the costs of Scheme 3 to determine the last line of the table, the incremental cash flows. The latter simply indicates that if the company puts up over the first four years the additional £3,553 which is required for Scheme 3 compared with Scheme 4, this will result in savings of £20,067 in year 5.

These cash flows can be evaluated quite simply by calculating the DCF return from investing the four 'capital' outlays of £3,553 to obtain

£20,067, having reduced all these sums to a net of tax basis using the 'Effective net of tax factor' from Table 2.8 explained in section 4 of Chapter 2. This return is the rate of discount r which gives:

$$(\text{Effective Net of Tax Factor}) \times$$
$$\left(\frac{£20,067}{(1+r)^5} - \frac{£3,553}{(1+r)^4} - \frac{£3,553}{(1+r)^3} - \frac{£3,553}{(1+r)^2} - \frac{£3,553}{(1+r)^1}\right) = 0$$

We can use the annuity factor (Table B) to compute the present value of the £3,553 for four years. Taking the tax rate as 50% and trying a 13% discount rate we get:

$$0·5838 \, (£20,067 \times 0·54276 - £3,553 \times 2·97447) = £189$$

(0·6670 is the net of tax factor from Table 2·8, 0·54276 is the 13% discount factor for five years, and 2·97447 is the 13% four year annuity factor from Table B).

Trying a 15% discount rate we get:

$$0·5946 \, (£20,067 \times 0·4971 - £3,553 \times 2·855) = -£100$$

Hence the DCF return is $13\% + 2\% \times £189/£289 = 14·3\%$. This means that the company can obtain 14·3% net of tax from the additional outlays required for Scheme 3 compared with Scheme 4. Return standards for virtually risk-free projects are set out in Chapter 4, section 1f. It is seen that by these standards the 14·3% is highly acceptable and on this basis Scheme 3 should be chosen in preference to Scheme 4.

The only remaining rental possibilities are now Schemes 2 and 3. We can evaluate these again by the incremental cash flow approach as shown in Table 6.6.

Table 6.6

Comparison of schemes 2 and 3

Schemes	Years				
	1	2	3	4	5
	£	£	£	£	£
3	24,504	24,504	24,504	24,504	884
2	30,948	30,948	30,948	884	884
Incremental cash flows (before tax)	−6,444	−6,444	−6,444	23,620	0

The incremental cash flows here indicate that Scheme 2 involves putting up £6,444 more over each of the first three years to save £23,620 in the fourth year: Again, regarding the additional outlay as a cost-saving investment and trying a 12% discount rate we get:

$$0.5782 \; (£23,620 \times 0.635518 - £6,444 \times 2.40183) = -£270.$$

Trying 10% we get:

$$0.5666 \; (£23,620 \times 0.683013 - £6,444 \times 2.48685) = £61.$$

Hence the DCF return is $10\% + 2\% \times 61/331 = 10.4\%$.

This level of return will also be generally acceptable on such a risk-free investment, and therefore sufficient justification for putting up the additional initial cost required for Scheme 2. The latter is therefore ascertained to be the best of the three leasing propositions.

c. General importance of incremental analysis

In this example the incremental cash flow approach has been used to determine the best of the leasing propositions. But precisely the same principle can be used to discriminate between different types of plant or contracts, or in any situation where a choice has to be made between competing schemes. This point is illustrated in Table 6.7. The choice here is between mutually exclusive alternatives A and B as regards size of plant.

Table 6.7

Choosing between mutually exclusive plants

Projects	Capital outlays	Annual cash flows Years 1 to 10	DCF returns
A	− £60,000	£14,310	20·0%
B	− £158,000	£32,690	16·0%
B − A	− £98,000	£18,380	13·4%

Project A costs £60,000 and has an annual net cash flow of £14,310 for ten years, and Project B costs £158,000 and has an annual net cash flow of £32,690 for ten years. The company is assumed to be looking for an 8% return on this category of investment. A has the higher return (20% compared with B's 16%), but the choice between mutually exclusive alternatives *cannot be made on the basis of these rates of return* (see section 1a of Chapter 11). Project B can be regarded as a 'package' consisting of Project A plus the project with the cash flows set out in the table as B – A. This package project thus *offers all that A has and in addition the project B – A*. The latter has a return of 13·4%. If this return is acceptable then Project B should be accepted.

In any incremental analysis, however, we need to take account of any exceptional risk to which the incremental cash flows are exposed. Thus if Project A were, say, a small-scale plant sufficient to supply an existing market but B was a larger plant to supply a larger market part of which the company had yet to secure, then the incremental cash flows are at an exceptionally high degree of risk—higher than those of A or B, for these cash flows are wholly contingent on securing additional markets. By isolating in this way the cash flows subject to exceptional degrees of risk, the incremental cash flow approach will often prove a useful step in analysing risk and the return being offered for risk bearing. Thus the question to be asked as regards the results of Table 6.7 is whether 13·4% is a sufficient return for the incremental risks attaching to the cash flows B – A. (The general problem of evaluating mutually exclusive projects is discussed in Section 1a of Chapter 11.)

3. Lease or buy

a. Basic method

Lease or buy situations arise very frequently in business. For instance, a great deal of industrial capital equipment can be leased as an alternative to purchase (as in the above computer example). Vehicles, ships and buildings are also very frequently the subject of lease transactions. The example now to be considered relates to the computer decision of Section 2 above.

It was decided from the analysis of that section that Scheme 2 was the best of the three leasing propositions. We now want to compare this with the outright purchase costing £88,400. This is best analysed as a straight cost-saving proposition. If the company purchases the computer outright it will cost £88,400, but save the rental payments that would otherwise have been incurred under Scheme 2. The relevant investment is therefore:

Years	0	1	2	3	4	5
Cash flows (before tax)	−£88,400	£30,948	£30,948	£30,948	£884	£884

where the three amounts of £30,948, and the two amounts of £884 are the annual amounts saved before tax.

In analysing these cash flows it will be desirable to take account of the fact that the cash flows of years 1 to 5 do not arise end year, but are spread over the whole year (the lease payments are actually quarterly in advance). This means on average they arise approximately mid-year, that is, half a year *earlier* than the end year average assumed with annual discounting. Normal discounting based on the convention that cash flows arise end year therefore 'overdoes' the discounting and need to be offset by multiplying the present value of the rental payments by $(1+r)^{\frac{1}{2}}$ where r is the DCF rate of return. (With low rates of discount the factor $(1+r)^{\frac{1}{2}}$ can be taken as equal to $1+\frac{r}{2}$. For a discussion of discounting on other than an end year basis see section 2 of Chapter 3.)

The choice between the three leasing schemes in section 2 should similarly have been made on the basis of mid-year discounting, but in this case the resulting returns would have been the same since the alternatives compared were all equally affected.

We now need to find the rate of discount that will make $-£88,400 +$ (present value grants and capital allowances) + (present value rental payments) × (the effective net of tax factor) × $(1+\frac{r}{2})$ equal to zero. The capital allowances are those indicated in column III of Table 2.8 and the tax rate is the 50% rate assumed in that table.

Trying 6% we get:

$$-£88,400 + (£88,400 \times 0·4582)$$
$$+ (£30,948 \times 2·6730 + £884 \times 1·8334 \times 0·8396) \times 0·5418 \times 1·03$$
$$= -£971$$

Trying 4% we get:

$$-£88,400 + (£88,400 \times 0·4714)$$
$$+ (£30,948 \times 2.7751 + £884 \times 1·8861 \times 0·8890) \times 0·5286 \times 1·02$$
$$= £377$$

Hence the DCF return is

$$4\% + \frac{2\% \times 377}{377 + 971} = 4·6\%$$

b. Conclusion

The project offers a return of 4·6% net of corporate tax in *money* terms. This return is virtually risk free since the savings are legally fixed. (The return, of course, depends on the tax rate, but it will be found that at this level the return would tend to increase with the tax rate owing to the effect of capital allowances.) Recommended rate of return standards for risk free investment were set out in Chapter 4, section 1f. In all cases it will be seen that, irrespective of the company's financing policy, this type of project will be unattractive and all companies should therefore reject the purchase alternative in favour of the Scheme 2 lease.

4. Major new project

This case study illustrates the presentation to senior management of a complex major project with particular reference to negotiating a sales contract to make the project viable. The example (based on an actual case) is of a mining project, but the essential technique is of general application.

a. Basic data

The project relates to a major copper orebody high in the mountains of South Island, New Zealand, fifty miles from the nearest rail connection closely linked to a sea port. The product of the mine is to be sold F.O.R. to a consortium of Japanese companies. The cost of the mine and all its associated facilities (a new road and an aerial ropeway) is estimated at £50 million. Owing to the mountainous terrain, however, it is not possible to guarantee the engineering estimates of either the road or the ropeway too closely, and the engineering consultants recommend that a further £10 million should be allowed to cover all contingencies. The total cost might therefore be as high as £60 million. While the engineering consultants consider that a capital overrun in excess of £60 million is most unlikely, in view of the size and importance of the project the directors of the sponsoring company require that all significant possibilities be evaluated, including the possibility that capital costs might be as high as £70 million. Construction time is estimated to be three years.

Subject to a satisfactory sales contract, a consortium of British and European banks, insurance companies, and finance houses, has agreed to finance 60% of the total capital cost up to £60 million, and the sponsoring company has guaranteed all necessary funds to complete the project to the extent that the cost is in excess of the £60 million.

The loan is to be at an 8% interest rate and repayable as a first charge on the net cash flow of the project. No dividends to shareholders are permitted until the loans are repaid in full. Working capital, estimated at £5 million once peak output is reached, is to be provided by New Zealand banks.

The company has several choices as regards its sales contract which is to be for a fifteen-year period. It can sell the first fifteen years' output of the mine at a price based on the annual world market price of electrolytic copper (the copper product the Japanese consortium will make from the mine's 40% copper concentrates), or it can negotiate a fixed price contract for either ten or fifteen years.

The world market price of copper is expected to average around £450 a ton for electrolytic copper over the first ten years of operation. What will happen beyond then can only be guessed at, although the best single estimate is that the average price will be significantly lower over the next decade as some loss of markets to cheaper metals and plastics is likely by then. The Japanese industrial consortium is willing to contract for the first ten years' mine output at a fixed price based on an electrolytic copper price of £400 a ton, and for a further five years at the then current world market price (i.e. each year's purchases in years eleven to fifteen would be based on annual average world market prices): this will be referred to as choice A. In choice B the Japanese will contract for the entire output of the mine for the first fifteen years of operation at a fixed price based on a £350 a ton electrolytic copper price. This lower price for the longer period reflects the expectation that copper prices will be weaker in the next decade, perhaps by a large margin. Choice C consists of using the average annual world copper price.

Virtually the whole of the capital in the project, with the exception of the working capital, is at risk in the sense that if the output of the mine is unsaleable for any reason almost none of the assets can be sold off for other uses. Further, the company has no other operations in New Zealand, so that the losses from the project cannot be written off against other taxable income. The sponsoring company would feel under a moral obligation to pay off the loan capital from other sources of income to the extent that the project could not do so, even though it would be under no *legal* obligation to do so—indeed, its future as a major company could be threatened if it did not so repay such loans to the best of its ability. In view of this the directors of the sponsoring company want the fairly sure prospect of their minimum equity DCF return of 9% on all the capital at risk, in this case, the total capital. This, in its essential form, is the basic data on which the sales negotiation should be based, and indeed the data needed to determine if the project is viable.[1] The problem now is to present this information in the form best suited to taking the appropriate decision. For ease of presentation no cognisance is taken of many other important considerations (the currency of the loan, what happens if there is devaluation, the effect of cost inflation in New Zealand, etc.) which arise in practice. Finally, even though the mine is likely to have an operational life well in excess of fifteen years, the profits of only the first fifteen years, the period of the firm sales contract, will be taken into account. Sales after that period will scarcely affect the DCF returns and so can safely be ignored in this case.

The relative magnitude of the sums involved and the uncertainty surrounding much of the data, in particular capital costs and selling price, necessitate a careful sensitivity analysis of the project to ascertain the range of outcomes from the different contractual choices, and what, if any, fail-safe choices exist.

b. Sensitivity analysis—the presentation of information for decision taking

The most satisfactory way of setting out all the significant combinations of this project is to make use of graphs and this is done in Figures 6.1, 6.2 and 6.3, each of which relate to a different capital cost and financing plan as shown in Table 6.8.

Table 6.8

Capital	Figure 6·1 (likely cost)	Figure 6·2 (likely maximum cost)	Figure 6·3 (highest cost worth considering)
	£m	£m	£m
Equity funds	20	24	34
Loan funds	30	36	36
Total cost	£50m	£60m	£70m

[1] In practice many complex problems would need to be resolved before the data could be in the form for negotiating a sales contract. These problems include the best way of mining the orebody which embraces the problem of choosing the most profitable annual rate of output, the problem of deciding in favour of both a road and an aerial ropeway, and the best routes for both, etc. All these problems should be resolved using optimising procedures based on discounting methods.

Fig 6·1

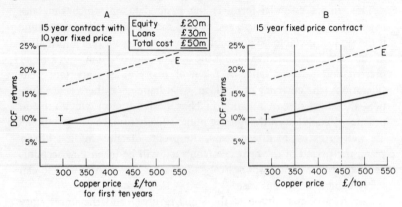

Fig 6·2

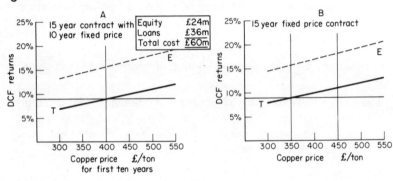

Fig 6·3

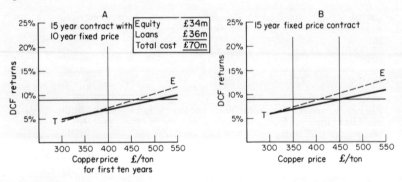

Each figure shows the DCF returns on both equity funds (dotted line marked E) and total funds (solid line marked T) for a range of electrolitic copper prices ranging from £300 to £550 a ton for the contract life of the first fifteen years of operations. Each figure is in two parts. The left hand parts (A) relate to the position for a ten year fixed price contract followed by a further five years during which the average contract price is based on electrolytic prices £100 a ton less than for the first ten years. The right hand parts (B) relate to the position where prices are constant over the whole fifteen years of the contract. Thus although both the A and B figures relate to specific fixed price contracts, both can be used to indicate the results of contracts where the price is based on world market prices. The A figures show the position if there is one average price for the first ten years followed by a £100 drop in the average price for the next five years. The B figures show the position for one average price over the whole fifteen years.

In practice the directors of the company would expect to see the forecast annual profit and net cash flow statements for half a dozen or so significant cases as well as these DCF figures, but in the interests of simplicity these accounting statements are not given here.

c. Interpretation of results

The interpretation of the results of the sensitivity analysis must be based on the consideration that the relative magnitude of the sums involved, the choice of contractual possibilities, and the uncertainty of much of the data all necessitate board consideration and evaluation. Even if the various outcomes could be assigned highly accurate probabilities, the full sensitivity analysis presentation would still be required since the consequences of the various outcomes are difficult to assess and different board members may evaluate them quite differently. Further, given all the risks involved in any course of action, it may well be desirable to forgo what may appear to be the likelihood of substantially greater returns for the security of lower but still acceptable returns.

The first point of interpretation to look for is the actual profitability of the project if the price of electrolytic copper is £450 a ton (the forecast average price for the first ten years of operation) for the whole of the first fifteen years of operation for the three different capital costs assuming the company elects to have choice C, a contract based on actual world annual copper prices. The results from the B figures are given in Table 6.9.

Table 6.9

Profitability of choice C for £450 a ton for fifteen years

Total capital cost	DCF return on total capital	DCF return on equity capital	Total equity capital
£50m	13%	22%	£20m
£60m	11%	18%	£24m
£70m	9%	10%	£34m

From this it is clear that the project would be attractively profitable for a capital cost of up to £60m, and marginal at £70m. (From the A figures similar results could be set out if the electrolytic copper price is £450 a ton for the first ten years and £350 for the next five years. The DCFs on total capital are about 1% down on the constant £450 a ton price, indicating that the breakeven capital would be £65m.)

The next step is to consider whether either of the fixed price contracts, choices A and B, might not be more attractive than choice C. Taking the capital cost at the likely expected maximum of £60m (Figure 6.2) it is seen that a fifteen-year contract at a price based on £350 a ton for electrolytic copper, choice B, gives a 9% DCF return on total capital, and nearly 16% on the equity capital. This result is clearly inferior to the non-fixed price contract (choice C) where the world market price averages (on a *discounted weighted* average basis) more than £350 a ton over the fifteen years. The choice between these two possibilities, B and C, will depend on the relative values the company's directors would attach to the prospects of the safer lower returns from the full fixed price contract compared with the chances of obtaining the significantly higher average returns based on the forecast prices for the next ten years (the years which mainly determine the DCFs). Further discussions with marketing experts would be called for on this point.

The third possibility, choice A, is the ten-year fixed price contract based on a £400 a ton price for electrolytic copper and world market prices for the next five years. It is apparent from the diagrams that a ten-year contract based on a £400 a ton electrolytic copper price would be better than a fifteen-year contract based on a £350 price providing the average world market price for the last five of the fifteen years is above £300 a ton.[1] Again, a decision would turn on the results of further discussions with marketing experts. If the marketing

---

[1] At £400 a ton for ten years and £300 a ton for five years the DCF returns are the same as for £350 a ton for fifteen years.

experts could hold out the reasonable likelihood of average prices in excess of £300 a ton for the last five of the fifteen years, then the ten years fixed price contract based on £400 a ton, choice A, is better than the fifteen-year fixed price contract on £350 a ton, choice B. The choice would then be between A (the ten-year fixed price contract), and C (the non-fixed price contract).[1]

In practice the full range of contract possibilities would not usually be known in advance, but would emerge during the course of negotiations, so figures of the type set out would actually be drawn up in final form only during the course of the negotiations, but their usefulness in helping to form opinion and decide on tactics and counter-offers during negotiations is obvious.

A final point to emerge from the figures is the exact consequences of capital costs being higher than forecast which can affect the decision on how much extra time and money it might be worth spending on engineering investigations and replanning to lower forecast costs, or gain advantages from being able to produce a higher output.

In presenting all this data we have not attempted to recommend how the decision should go, for that depends on value judgments. Rather we have attempted to show how the right presentation of the data can help those with the responsibility for the decision.

[1] The three contract choices, A, B and C are, of course, mutually exclusive. For this reason it can sometimes be misleading, as is set out in section 2c above, to base a decision entirely on the separate DCF returns. Resort must often be had also to the incremental DCF returns, etc. Where the normal DCF returns are insufficient, it is the analysts' duty to draw this fact to the attention of senior management and to provide any requisite additional analysis. In the example under consideration here, however, no such additional information is required— the decision can be taken satisfactorily on the basis of the normal DCF returns of the separate possibilities.

7

The basic analysis of replacement investments

1. Introduction

Replacement investments differ from other investments primarily in that they involve the displacement or scrapping of existing capital assets. Many investment decisions which are mainly related to expansion may, however, involve an element of replacement if the new asset required for expansion is found capable of performing some of the services provided by existing assets. Because there is therefore no clearcut distinction between replacement investment and non-replacement investment, it is impossible to give any accurate assessment of its relative importance compared with other types of investment, but it is probable that investment mainly related to replacement accounts for at least half of all private corporate investment. It is, therefore, of very considerable national importance that replacement decisions should be analysed in the most efficient way possible.

Detailed surveys (see reference 2 of Chapter 9) have shown that this category of decisions, like most investment decisions in Britain, is undertaken on the basis of criteria which are highly inadequate and fall very far short of the best available methods. It is also probable that replacement decisions are subject to even less searching appraisal than are investments for expansion, since the latter tend to be relatively more simple and are encouraged by the generally expansionist philosophy of business. As replacement investments are generally more complicated to analyse and lack the glamour of expansion investments, they tend to fall victim to the lack of attention and attitude of general conservatism shown to cost saving investments.

In this chapter we consider the basic factors involved in replacement investment decisions. Because of the inherent complexity of optimising the timing and profitability of replacement investments, it is recommended that, after understanding the principles outlined here, the reader consults the references given at the end of the chapter for a more comprehensive treatment.

2. Fundamentals of replacement analysis

a. The basic questions

Replacement decisions turn on answering essentially the same questions as any other capital expenditure, namely the following:

(i) Having regard to the overall profitability *of the activity* in question, is it worth making any new investment at all? If the answer is that replacement is out of the question, then the only problem is whether the existing asset should be scrapped now or at some future date. If, however, the activity is sufficiently profitable to justify further investment then the following questions relating to type and timing of new investment need to be answered.

(ii) What is the optimal economic life of the new investment?

(iii) When is the best time to make the new investment? (What is the *optimal time* to scrap the existing asset and instal the replacement?)

(iv) What is the profitability on the new investment compared with going on with the old asset?

In replacement analysis the answers to these fundamental questions are particularly complicated. The first question involves determining what the incremental cash flows would be if the existing asset was scrapped immediately and not replaced. In the majority of cases it will usually be apparent that it will always pay to have some asset performing the function rather than none. More important, and more difficult to answer are questions (ii) and (iii) which involve a careful balancing of the changing costs and revenues of successive generations of assets against capital costs. A decision to prolong the life of an existing asset involves sacrificing the immediately greater earning power of a new asset in order to postpone the capital outlay required to obtain this asset. It also involves allowing for the fact that the longer replacement is postponed, the greater is the possibility that some improved model will become available with even greater earning power than the existing new models. Question (iv) turns on the answers to the other questions and can involve considering several generations of assets. Finally, it is essential to consider the possibilities for expansion which are offered by the replacement decision. In sum, we need simultaneously the answers to all the questions listed above for all the possible investment opportunities.

b. Method of approach

In order to begin to solve these problems satisfactorily it is necessary to start with some basic method of investment appraisal which is capable of reflecting adequately all the complicated factors entering into the decision. In particular, it is necessary to take account of the timing and variation in receipts and outlays as well as the very important grants and tax concessions on almost all types of industrial capital equipment. Only the discounting methods, which take the actual cash outlays and inflows over the years into account, are capable of solving all the problems of replacement decisions.

Having decided on the basic line of approach, the next point to be decided with replacement decisions, as with any other investment decision, is the basis for comparison. In a straightforward expansion investment we would simply calculate what a company obtains in actual cash inflows and outflows over the life of an investment compared with the alternative of doing nothing, hence, making no outlay and obtaining no receipts. In the case of a replacement investment the first calculation is whether a company would be better off scrapping its existing asset either at once or when it comes to the end of its life, and not replacing it at all. This is usually straightforward enough. As long as the existing asset makes some contribution to profit above its cash costs it is worth keeping on until this is no longer true rather than scrapping it without replacement. Then it has to be decided if a replacement at that time is going to result in cash flows to give an adequate DCF return on its capital cost.

It will usually be obvious from even rough calculations that a replacement at some time will be better than nothing so the usual comparison in replacement investments will be between replacing the existing asset at once or some time over the next few years.

Suppose that it is clear that replacement at some time will be justified and that the problem is to determine whether replacement should be immediate or postponed. Assume the existing asset will be contributing £100 a year of net cash flows to a company for two more years after which it will break down completely, while a new asset costing £1,000 would contribute an annual net cash flow of £433 for four years before breaking down. Assuming no technical progress on future models and a zero resale value on the existing machine whenever it is scrapped, when should replacement take place, at once or in two years' time? As with any other investment decision, this requires an analysis of the relevant *incremental* net cash flows which are set out in Table 7.1.

Table 7.1

Annual cash flows of a replacement investment

Years	0	1	2	3	4	5	6	7	8
Cash flows £									
1. Replacement now	− 1,000	433	433	433	− 1,000 433	433	433	433	− 1,000 433
2. Replacement in year 2	—	100	− 1,000 100	433	433	433	− 1,000 433	433	433
3. Incremental net cash flows (1) − (2)	− 1,000	333	1,333	0	− 1,000	0	1,000	0	− 1,000

The incremental net cash flows set out in line 3 of the table result from subtracting the cash flows involved in replacement in two years' time and every four years thereafter, from the similar cash flows resulting from immediate replacement. This example illustrates that replacing now instead of at the end of two years creates a long chain of altered incremental cash flows, some positive and some negative, over all the future years that the company employs this type of asset.

c. DCF return on the incremental cash flows

We now need to calculate the DCF return which these cash flows will produce on the initial − £1,000 of year zero. The calculation involves some difficulty because of the continuing nature of the cash flows and so the discounting is best performed in two stages, taking first all the cash flows after year 2. Let us assume that the series of − £1,000 and + £1,000 after year 2 go on for ever and try to evaluate the present value at the end of year 2 of all these cash flows. Consider first the positive cash flows, i.e. the £1,000 which on our assumptions will occur at four yearly intervals for ever.

The present value of any regular sum £X per period for ever is simply this amount divided by the rate of interest *appropriate to that period*. Thus the present value of £100 per annum for ever discounted at 10% is simply £100/0·10 = £1,000. In our case the amount is £1,000 for ever at *four yearly* intervals. The four yearly rate of interest equivalent to a one year rate of r is $(1+r)^4 - 1$. For example, if the interest rate is 10% per annum then $r = ·10$ and the corresponding four year interest rate will be $(1·10)^4 - 1 = ·464$. The present value at the end of year 2 of all the cash flows of $+£1,000$ at four yearly intervals is therefore £1,000/·464 = £2,155.

The negative cash flows are simply the same series but *negative* rather than positive and occurring two years *earlier*. Hence, their present value is $-£2,155 \times 1·10^2$ where the $1·10^2$ is simply 'offsetting' the two years of excessive discounting involved in the £2,155 present value. Adding these two components of present value together we see that the net present value at the end of year 2 is £2,155 - £2,608 = -£453. This present value must always be negative at any positive rate of discount, because the negative cash flows always precede the positive and hence must have the higher present value. Now the DCF approach is essentially meaningless when applied to situations of this kind (see section 1a of Chapter 11). This is because the series of alternate $-£1,000$ and $+£1,000$ represents a *net liability*. It represents a commitment to lay out £1,000 every four years (beginning in year 4) just to get back £1,000 two years later. As long as money has any time value, that is as long as the discount rate is positive, this must represent a liability. To allow for this *we must, in fact, discount this series at the company's normal cost of capital*. If this is taken as 8% we get the present value of this series as $£1000/(1·08^4 - 1) - £1000 \times 1·08^2/(1·08^4 - 1) = -£462$. This $-£462$ is the present value at end year 2 of all the cash flows after year 2. We now deduct this sum from the cash flows in year 2 of £1,333 to get £1,333 - £462 = £871. This treatment of the cash flows after year 2 can be regarded as making a provision out of the positive cash flow of year 2 in order to meet the liability which the project constitutes after that date. With this adjustment the series of cash flows in Table 7.1 is as shown in Table 7.2.

Table 7.2

Years	0	1	2
Adjusted incremental cash flows	-£1,000	£333	£871

The normal DCF computation is then applied to these cash flows and the return is found to be 11·5%.

Subject to the adjustment to take account of the net liability which the project becomes after year 2, this DCF return has all its normal significance. In this example the 11·5% is the DCF return on the incremental cash flows from replacing now rather than in two years' time. This can be interpreted as meaning (see Table 7.2) that the company obtains 11·5% over these two years after providing for all the financial disadvantage (the −£462) arising in subsequent years. *It therefore indicates the attractiveness of replacing immediately rather than in two years' time.*

In actual replacement appraisals allowance must be made for other cash flows: for example, changing operating costs on the old or new asset, changing levels of earnings and possible improvements in earnings in each successive replacement. While these other factors vary the patterns of the cash flows, they do no more than complicate the arithmetic. It must be stressed that the essential principle and method of the calculation is simply that illustrated above.

Following this basic line of approach we are now in a position to see the figures which we require in order to make our optimal replacement decisions.

d. Answers to basic questions (ii) (iii) and (iv)

(i) *Optimal timing and whole life return*

Assuming for the moment that we already know the optimal life of the replacement (the answer to question (ii) above) we must next consider the best time to make the investment (the answer to question (iii)), that is the best time to scrap the existing asset and introduce the replacement. This question of timing is of fundamental importance. The new asset should be introduced just as soon as its additional earnings are sufficient in the first year of its life to provide an adequate return on the capital expenditure involved. (The exceptional costs—such as running-in expenses, etc.—are really in the nature of once and for all outlays and should therefore be excluded from earnings in the first year and added to the capital cost of the machine.) This amounts to saying that the asset should be replaced as soon as the rate of return on the above basis of calculation is sufficient to provide an adequate minimum rate of return. Whilst it is superficially attractive to leave replacement until the additional earnings have become so substantial that the asset earns a high rate of return in the first year, it should be clear that this is not an economically sound policy since the price of this high return will have been years of earnings forgone that would have adequately met the required rate of return.

Hence, our question (iii) above can be rephrased as the alternative question: what is the rate of return from the replacement over its first year? The basis of this return is essentially that given in the above example except that the comparison is between replacing now rather than in *one* year's time (not two years' time as in Table 7.1). If this return is not adequate then we should not plan to replace. If, on the other hand, this return does seem to be adequate, we should then ask question (iv), namely, what is the return from the replacement over the whole period of its life? This is essentially asking the question, what is the return from replacing now rather than going on with the old asset for a period equal to the whole life of a new replacement? It may seem that this question is redundant since if the increasing costs of the old machine make it profitable to replace it now rather than wait even a year, it must be the case that it will not pay to continue running the old machine for a period as long as the optimal life of a new and improved machine. But returns from postponing replacement over the whole life of a new asset provide a useful upper limit from which the returns from shorter postponement periods can be estimated. These returns indicate the extent to which longer term postponement is economically viable and hence may assist decision taking where, for intangible reasons or suspected inaccuracy of the data, some decision takers are not sufficiently convinced by the one or two year comparisons, and feel that replacement should be postponed for some longer period.

(ii) Optimal life

There remains to be considered the question of optimal life of the initial replacement asset. It should be apparent on reflection that the optimal life of the replacement will be determined by precisely the same sort of circumstances as are being used to determine the optimal date to terminate the life of the existing asset. The life of the replacement therefore stretches out to the point at which it, in its turn, is superseded by its replacement which can show additional earnings such that they are sufficient to give an adequate return and pay for its decline in value over the first year of operation.

References

General Reference
(A) Chapter 20
Special References
1. H. G. THUBYSEN. *Engineering Economy*, Prentice Hall, 1957.
2. GEORGE M. TERBORGH, *Business Investment Policy*, Machinery and Allied Products Institute, 1959.
3. J. CONNOR and J.B. EVANS. *Replacement Investment*, Gower Press, 1972.

8

Evaluating companies for acquisition

The whole of this chapter is concerned with techniques for assessing corporate acquisition prospects: in the first part of the chapter are summarised the key items which should be evaluated when assessing the value of an acquisition possibility; in the second the conventional methods of approach, using price/earnings multiples and earnings per share, are considered; and in the final part an extension of the earnings per share approach is described. The entire subject is discussed in Reference A, Chapters 10, 11 and 12, to which readers are recommended to refer for fuller discussion and examples.

1. The basic principles

The merger with or acquisition of another company is essentially another type of investment project, albeit a particularly complex one. As such, mergers and takeovers must satisfy the same criteria and be judged on the same grounds as any other investments open to a company. DCF and risk analysis techniques, etc., are as applicable to this type of investment as to replacements, internal expansions, or leasing projects. The purchase of an existing company, however, usually involves many special problems or problems at a greater level of complexity than commonly occur with internal investments. These complexities, coupled with the fact that such projects are usually by far the most costly of all investments, require that special attention should be given to company acquisition and mergers.

Amongst the many special factors to be considered, the following are particularly important. First, the cost of (or in the case of a merger, the value to be placed on) the company concerned will not usually be known in advance: instead a range of prices will have to be worked out in advance of negotiation. Second, the means of payment will need careful evaluation whenever it is intended or contemplated that all or part of the purchase price is to be in the form of the purchasing company's own shares. Third, purchase may bring with it the opportunity to raise further debt capital on the assets of the purchased company or alternatively, the requirement to pay off its debts and legal obligations. Fourth, mergers and takeovers usually involve many special tax complexities, indeed tax considerations may constitute the prime reasons for the merger or acquisition.

The basic information required for an acquisition or merger can be listed under four headings.

(i) Future profits

The most appropriate source for data for giving initial guidance in preparing these estimates is the Bid-for company's published accounts over the past few years. Trends in revenue, costs and earnings should be carefully studied, together with accompanying notes and statements, to collect pointers to future developments. Adjustments should be made to the trends to allow for changes in the company's assets—especially if these have resulted from take-overs—and for inflation, so that the real earnings performance of the company can be revealed. The industry in which the company's activities play a part should be analysed to determine trends which might affect the purchased company and to assess its competitiveness. Any extraordinary events in the company's or industry's recent past performance should be identified and the trends adjusted for these.

(ii) Replacements

Estimates of the timing and amounts of all *essential* replacement expenditures should be made. This is a difficult task when considering only the published information relating to a company; however, company statements and reports generally contain considerable useful indications of the scale of total capital expenditure, of the date of installation of major assets whose lives can then be assessed, of depreciation provisions and movements in book asset values, and so on.

(iii) Surplus assets

Estimates should be prepared of the values of all surplus assets— that is, all assets not required to earn the profits forecast under (i).

Such assets comprise surplus cash and investments—often detectable from analysis of balance sheets and cash statements—unused land and surplus buildings, and so on. Again useful hints can be found in reports, Press comments, and the like, although this is an area where accuracy of forecasting cannot be expected.

(iv) Debt position

Estimates can be derived from balance sheet information of the amount and timing of debt and loan redemption plus renewal possibilities, plus the likely scope for raising additional debt.

These four categories of data contain the basic information necessary for the evaluation of a company. Items (i), (ii) and (iv) give the *equity* net cash flow from the new investment. When this equity net cash flow is discounted at the Bidder company's equity cost of capital, and the value of any surplus assets (iii) is added, the resulting total is the maximum value of the company. This approach brings out the essential fact that apart from any surplus assets the value of the acquisition cannot exceed *the net cash flow which the purchaser can get out of it*. Thus if the new company is to be expanded so that most or all of its internally generated funds must be reinvested to produce the higher profits of later years, then it would be double counting to take credit for the profits of both the early and later years. Only the actual net cash flowing to the purchaser is relevant to the valuation.

The essential nature of the DCF analysis as applied to acquisitions or mergers is shown in the numerical example of Table 8.1 in which the company acquired is assumed to have no significant scope for raising additional debt capital but considerable surplus cash and other assets.

Table 8.1 (£000's)

Source of net cash flow	Years 0	1	2	3	4	5	6 onwards
1. Surplus assets	0	0	300	0	0	0	0
2. Dividends (gross)	0	600	270	300	320	360	Growing from £360 in year 5 by 4% per annum
3. Present value at year 5 of dividends of year 6 onwards	—	—	—	—	—	6,000	—
4. = 1 + 2 + 3	0	600	570	300	320	6,360	—

In this case the Bidder company intends to dispose of £300,000 of the surplus assets of the acquisition and to pay special dividends over the first few years to absorb some of the acquired company's surplus cash. (It is here assumed that the Bid-For company remains in being and that the only way to get cash out is via dividends.) With various other economies and a change in the Bid-For company's distribution policy to pay out future excess cash generation, the dividends paid to the new parent company will be as shown in the table for years 1 to 5. For the following years dividend policy will be set to absorb future surplus cash generated, but it is thought that the balance retained can be profitably invested and will produce a growth of dividends of 4% per annum from an initial level of £360,000 in year 5. Assume a 10% cost of capital.

This continuing stream of dividends from year 6 onwards can be brought to its present value in year 5 simply by dividing the initial sum (the £360,000 of year 5) by the discount rate less the rate of growth —that is $\cdot 10 - \cdot 04 = \cdot 06$ (essentially the growth offsets the discounting). This makes the present value in year 5 of the dividend stream arising after year 5 equal to £360,000/·06 = £6m. (The method of discounting a perpetual series is given in reference A 1.) The amounts to be brought to their present value at time zero are therefore the sums shown in the last row of the Table 8.1, and at a 10% discount rate, these have a present value of £5·410m. If the Bidder company pays this amount in *cash* for the acquisition it will obtain a 10% net of corporate tax return on its investment. The return for different purchase prices can be ascertained by determining the discount rates which bring the present values of future cash flows into equality with the various possible purchase prices.

Where it is proposed to acquire the company for a consideration which is not wholly cash—for example, issue of shares or debentures— the analysis will have to be extended to take into account the true cost of these to the acquiring company. The cost of issuing shares is unlikely to be the same as their valuation by the market, and indeed, once the new shares have been issued and the two companies combined, it will be coincidental for the share price to remain unchanged. The real cost of the newly issued shares will be the present value of all the dividends which the acquiring company believes it will have to pay on them. This, of course, includes dividends paid out of earnings which are already being generated within the acquiring company, and which will now be partly owned by the shareholders of the acquired company. In other words, the existing shareholders of the acquiring company are giving up a share of their present business in order to obtain a share in a new business. Care will have to be taken at this point to ensure that the forecast *total* dividends are sensible in relation to the forecast *total*—that is, post-acquisition—earnings of the company, and do not simply reflect pre-acquisition earnings. The present value of these dividends should then result in a figure not far different from the 'market' value attached to the shares issued in the purchase of the acquired company, since a present value of dividends significantly below this level implies either continued capital appreciation of the shares—reflected in reinvested cash which in turn should be forecast eventually to produce greater dividends—or failure to provide the return which the new shareholders would expect—which in the long run would impair the company's financial standing.

Similarly the cost of issuing debt as part of a purchase package is the present value of the after-tax interest payments and of the re-payment cash flows, allowing for the real diminution of these obligations over time as the impact of inflation increases. In evaluating the purchase of a company where a substantial proportion of the consideration takes the turn of debt or convertibles it will be found that the real cost of the purchase to the acquiring company is significantly below that if the bid were composed solely of cash.

2. Commonly used shortest methods

The two most commonly used methods of acquisition appraisal are the purchase price earnings multiple (P/E) and the earnings per share (EPS) methods. Both are relatively simple and can best be described in terms of the hypothetical examples shown in Table 8.2. In this simple example the Bidder Company whose shares stand at 180p makes a bid for the Bid-For Company whose shares stand at 120p. This bid is for shares and involves the offer of two Bidder Company shares for every three Bid-For Company shares. If the offer were accepted it would involve therefore the issue of six million more shares of the Bidder Company, making its total shares in issue 16 million. The total consideration involved in the bid is then this six million shares which have a current market value of £10·8 million.

The forecast earnings of the two companies for the year immediately following on the acquisition are also shown in Table 8.2. From this it is seen that the Bidder Company will obtain £0·90 million for its £10·8 million of shares, so that the price earnings multiple or 'exit' P/E of the acquisition is 12. (This compares with the Bidder Company's own price earnings multiple shown in the table as 15.) The acquisition would therefore be described as being on a P/E of 12, and this ratio would be compared with that of the acquiring company and possibly other companies which might be acquired to gauge its relative attractiveness.

The earnings per share of the two companies pre-bid and for the Bidder Company post-bid are also shown in the table. It is seen that the Bidder Company's earnings per share post-bid will be 13·12p compared with 12·0p pre-bid, so that the bid will have brought about an improvement in earnings per share of 1·12p. Providing then that there is not a corresponding proportionate decline in the price earnings multiple of the Bidder Company, the bid must improve the prospects of the Bidder Company in this first year (in fact the share price would rise to 197p compared with 180p if the price earnings multiple remained at its pre-bid level of 15). In the acquisition criterion attention would then focus on the level of improvement in EPS relative to other factors, such as uncertainties attaching to the future earnings estimates, possible adverse effects on the P/E, etc.

It might also be noted that in this example the improvement in earnings per share in the first year is brought about wholly by the difference in the price earnings multiples of the two companies (15 compared with 12). Insofar as the Bidder Company has no better earnings growth than that of the companies it acquired, so that its exceptional growth in EPS simply results from making acquisitions on the basis of its higher price earnings multiple, this would be an example of the so-called 'chain-letter' type of acquisition.

Each of the two statistics, the purchase P/E and the EPS, answer different questions. The purchase P/E indicates the multiple of earnings for which the acquiring company is paying. Its usefulness is mainly in terms of comparison with its own price earnings multiple and that which might have to be paid for alternative acquisitions; in other words, it is an indicator of the relative cheapness or dearness of the acquisition. Given, however, that it is by definition a multiple of only the *first* year earnings of the acquisition, it needs to be interpreted with some care with due allowance made for future growth of earnings by both the acquired and the acquiring companies.

The earnings per share statistic answers an entirely different question, namely that of the increase in earnings per share of the existing shareholders of the acquiring company. It is clearly important that consideration is given to this statistic since it will normally be a prior condition of the bid bringing about an improvement in the acquiring company share price that it can also bring about an improvement in its earnings per share.

Table 8.2

EPS method of aquisition analysis

	Bidder	Bid For	Bidder Post-Bid
Net earnings	£1·2m	£0.90m	£2·1m
Shares in issue	10m	9m	16m
EPS	12p	10p	13·12p
Price per share	180p	120p	197p
Price earnings ratio	15	12	15

As methods of assessing the attractiveness of acquisitions both methods obviously need considerable amplification and interpretation to allow for other relevant factors. Neither method, for example, takes account of the growth of earnings after the first year. Similarly, the purchase P/E method takes no account of the way in which the bid is being financed, although it has been shown to have a considerable bearing on the attractiveness of the investment whether the consideration is equity, debt, or cash. Further, a major problem in using the P/E method of assessing acquisitions is that insofar as the acquisition involves the issue of additional shares it raises the crucial problem of the method by which the shares are to be valued. It is clearly of fundamental importance whether the shares so issued are under- or over-valued relative to their market price at the time of acquisition. Moreover, the very fact of the acquisition being generally unexpected and its consequences not being generally known to the stock market will tend to cause the shares of the acquiring company to be either under- or over-valued.

The earnings per share approach has the considerable advantage of circumventing the problem of attaching a valuation to the company's shares. In its computation—as was seen in Table 8.2—the share price is never directly considered. The practical problems of this approach are, firstly, those of extending its scope to take into account other factors, such as that of the cash or gearing potential of the acquisition and, secondly, having to extend the method to provide convenient measures for assessing the effect of the acquisition on the acquiring company's P/E ratio, and consequently clearer acceptance criteria. The need for such criteria is apparent from the fact that the size of the increase in earnings per share cannot itself be an adequate criterion for accepting the acquisition, since it will depend on the relative size of the company being acquired: a small increase in the earnings per share might in no way reflect adversely upon the attractiveness of the acquisition, but simply on the fact that the acquisition is relatively small compared with the acquiring company.

3. The earnings per share ratio

The earnings per share ratio approach to acquisition is a method of extending the usefulness of the traditional EPS approach. The technique can be illustrated by a simple extension of the previous example, the salient characteristics of the extended version being shown in Table 8.3. In this the Bidder Company, besides issuing 6 million shares, also offers £1 million cash, and £1 million of loan stock with an 8% coupon, convertible between the second and the fifth years following the acquisition at a price of 200p per share (compared with the current 180p).

In the table both the convertible and cash are treated as simply giving rise to an interest charge of £0·08 million (8% of £2 million less tax relief of 50% from the assumed corporation tax of 50%). This is on the assumption that the only cash consequence of raising the loan is the interest charge—that is, the company is not obliged to pass up other worthwhile investment opportunities for want of cash.

The forecast growth of earnings of the Bidder Company is shown in the first line of the table, and that of the Bid-For Company in the following three lines. Under the heading 'Synergy' is represented cost savings, etc., arising from the combination of the two companies. In the line shown as 'Interest Saved' we also take into account some disposals of assets resulting in cash gains. These are assumed

Table 8.3

Earnings per share ratio (Net of Corporation Tax Basis)

	Years	1	2	3	4
Earnings: Bidder		1·20	1·50	1·80	1·85
Bid-For		0·90	0·95	1·00	1·30
£m Synergy		—	0·10	0·20	0·28
Interest incurred		(0·08)	(0·08)	(0·08)	(0·04)
Interest saved				0·12	0·16
Bidder Post Bid		2·02	2·47	3·04	3·55
Shares in issue		16m	16m	16m	16·5m
EPS Post-Bid		12·62p	15·44p	19·00p	21·51p
pence Pre-Bid (10m shares only)		12·00p	15·00p	18·00p	18·50p
EPS Gain		0·62p	0·44p	1·00p	3·01p
Old shareholders earnings: A. Gained £m		0·56	0·65	0·82	1·05
B. Ceded £m		0·50	0·61	0·72	0·75
EPSR		1·12	1·07	1·13	1·40

$$\text{EPSR} = \frac{\text{Earnings gained by old shareholders}}{\text{Earnings ceded and interest costs incurred by old shareholders}}$$

In Year 1, EPSR =

$$\frac{0·62 \times 10m + £1·20m \times \frac{6}{16} + £0·08m \times \frac{10}{16}}{£1·20 \times \frac{6}{16} + £0·08m \times \frac{10}{16}} = \frac{£0·56m}{£0·50m} = 1·12$$

In Year 4, EPSR =

$$\frac{3·01p \times 10m + £1·85m \times \frac{6·5}{16·5} + £0·04m \times \frac{10}{16·5}}{£1·85m \times \frac{6·5}{16·5} + £0·04m \times \frac{10}{16·5}} = \frac{£1·05m}{£0·75m} = 1·40$$

to amount to £3·0m in the year 3, and are treated as effectively reducing bank borrowing at 8% and so increasing earnings by £0·12m net of corporation tax at the assumed level of 50%.

In year 4 further rationalisation is assumed to produce cash of £1m and further interest savings of £0·04m net of corporation tax. In the same year the convertible is assumed to be converted and to result in an increase of the shares in issue of 0·5 million but with compensating interest savings of £0·04m leaving the net 'interest incurred' burden as £0·04m.

The subsequent calculations giving rise to the gain in earnings per share of the acquiring company in the table are self-evident. The gain in earnings per share is seen to be 0·62p in the first year and after falling to 0·44p in the second rising to 3·01p in year 4.

The earnings per share ratio given in the last line is defined at the foot of the table. Effectively it computes the total gain in earnings by the acquiring company's old shareholders (that is the shareholders prior to the acquisition), as a proportion of the total earnings which these old shareholders have ceded to the shareholders of the company which they have acquired and the interest charges which they have incurred. In the first year, for example, the old shareholders, as a result of the increase in the share capital by 6 million shares to 16 million shares, cede 6/16 of the £1·2m (£0·45m) which their old company expects to earn in the first year, and take on payment of 10/16 of the £0·08m (£0·05m) of interest payments for the cash and convertible—a total of £0·50m. *If no earnings materialise as a result of this acquisition this £0·50m will be the total sum which will have been sacrificed out of the earnings of that year. Hence it is the sum which can be regarded as the sum at stake.*

The gain from the acquisition to the old shareholders is effectively the recovery of this £0·50m sum, plus additional savings of 0·62p per share × 10 million shares = £0·062m, a total of £0·562m. The resulting EPSR is 0·562/0·5, or 1·12—a 12% gain.

The ratio therefore reflects the potential gain relative to what is at stake for the company's existing shareholders, effectively what most rates of return on investments endeavour to show. By representing the acquisition in this form rather than simply the increase in earnings per share we circumvent the difficulty already referred to, namely that an acquisition may give rise to only a modest increase in earnings per share despite being highly attractive simply because the acquisition is small compared with the already existing size of the acquiring company.

Casting the acquisition in this ratio form is also convenient in terms of taking into account the sometimes fairly intangible characteristic of the 'quality' of the earnings ceded compared with those acquired. Thus, if the acquiring company were in an industry thought of as having relatively high quality of earnings (say the fairly stable financial sector) while the company acquired was in a less favoured sector (say the volatile holiday tour business) the earnings per share ratio would have to be of a magnitude that reflected the relative quality of the two types of earnings. Thus in this example, the holiday tour earnings would ultimately (by year 4) have to be rated at more than $1 \cdot 4$ to every one of the financial sector earnings if the acquisition was not likely to have so adverse an effect upon the price earning multiple of the acquiring company.

In the example in Table 8.3 the major benefits of the acquisition are relatively long delayed—i.e. to year 4 when the EPSR rises to $1 \cdot 4$. Insofar as useful estimates can be compiled that far into the future it would be desirable to continue the calculations of the ratio until such time as it achieves stability (here taken to be year 4), thus reflecting the full impact of the acquisition.

4. Discounted EPSR

The analysis so far has been in terms of the short term effects of an acquisition. By its very nature, however, an acquisition is bound to have a very long term impact and it is against this that the short term effects must be weighed. The long term comparison can be conducted in terms of earnings using the 'discounted EPSR' defined as follows:

$$\frac{\text{Discounted earnings acquired by old shareholders}}{\text{Discounted earnings ceded and interest incurred by old shareholders}}$$

where the discount rate is that which shareholders apply to equity earnings and dividends. The only additional complexity in this calculation is the growth rate assumed to apply after the period in which the EPSR stabilises (year 4 in the example of Table 8.3), for which we recommend making explicit assumptions about future growth rates. As is shown in Reference A1, £1 growing in perpetuity at a rate of g per annum and discounted at the rate of r has a present value

$$P = \frac{1}{r_0} \quad \text{where} \quad r_0 = \frac{r-g}{1+g}$$

Hence the present value in year ZERO of the earnings stream after the stabilisation year would be $Pv_{m|r}$, where m is the year of stabilisation. The discounted EPSR is therefore

$$\frac{A_1 v_{1|r} + A_2 v_{2|r} \dots P A_m v_{m|r}}{B_1 v_{1|r} + B_2 v_{2|r} \dots P B_m v_{m|r}}$$

where the A_i are the 'Old Shareholders' Earnings Gained', and the B_i are the 'Old Shareholders' Earnings Ceded' as shown in Table 8.3, while P can be $1/r_0$ as derived from the growth formula.

Taking $r = 0 \cdot 10$ (i.e. a 7% discount rate in *real* terms + a 3% expected inflation rate) and $r_0 = 0 \cdot 06$ (giving a 16·7 P/E) the example of Table 8.3 has a discounted EPSR of

$$\frac{£0 \cdot 56m \times 0 \cdot 909 + £0 \cdot 65m \times 0 \cdot 826 + £0 \cdot 82m \times 0 \cdot 751 + 16 \cdot 7 \times £1 \cdot 05m \times 0 \cdot 683}{£0 \cdot 50m \times 0 \cdot 909 + £0 \cdot 61m \times 0 \cdot 826 + £0 \cdot 72m \times 0 \cdot 751 + 16 \cdot 7 \times £0 \cdot 75m \times 0 \cdot 683} = 1 \cdot 36$$

The interpretation of this ratio is that it represents the present value of earnings acquired by the old shareholders for every unit of present value of future earnings which they cede. While of necessity it involves assessing the shareholders' discount rate r and the long term growth rate g, these enter into both the numerator and denominator of the ratio with the consequence that the ratio is not particularly sensitive to their precise values.

The discounted EPSR can be regarded as the ultimate criterion of the acquisition in the sense that, if this is sufficiently large, it must compensate either for any adverse differences in the quality of earnings or adverse EPSRs in the early years. As regards the latter, it may be worth recalling that for a mature company which has ultimately relatively good growth prospects, (as evidenced by a high discounted EPSR), there are usually a number of ways in which short term earnings can be enhanced—albeit possibly at the cost of earnings in the future. Examples of this would be short term stringency in manning standards, checks on the recruitment of more staff, a slowing down of the rate of internal expansion where this involves short term adverse effects on profit, etc. Hence in the majority of profit motivated *acquisitions* (as compared with size motivated *mergers*), the major consideration is likely to be the level of the discounted EPSR relative to the intangible of the quality of the earnings gained and the risks inherent in the imperfect knowledge which applies to almost all acquisitions.

9

The conventional methods of investment appraisal

This chapter considers the two most commonly used conventional methods of investment appraisal, 'payback' and the 'accountant's' or 'book rate of return'. The suitability of these methods compared with the more rigorous but somewhat more complex discounting methods will be examined in some detail since if the conventional methods were sufficiently accurate for most practical purposes (as is still widely believed) then there would be little point in using more complex methods. This, as will be demonstrated, is not the case. The conventional methods are generally seriously inadequate approximations to the discounting methods and must frequently result in substantially suboptimal investment decisions. Their simplicity of application will be seen to arise from their lack of realism in the practical context of investment appraisal.

1. Payback[1]

a. Definition and use

Payback is the most commonly used method of investment appraisal in Britain. Some 78% (see references 1 and 2) of companies were found to be using this method in 1964/5. Of this 78%, some 96% used it *gross of tax*, so that the payback investment criterion was in effect the number of years before the gross of tax cash flows from the project equalled its capital cost.

The number of years to payback which the surveyed companies were looking for varied considerably, with 17% looking for a payback of three

---

[1] Reference A7, Section 2.

years, 17% for four years, 24% for five years, 11% for six years and 6% for seven years.

b. Rationale

The first question to be asked is the objective of the payback approach and second the extent to which this objective is relevant and useful. If the objective is to reflect the relative financial attractiveness of projects then it is very ineffective. This is illustrated in Table 9·1 which shows the net of tax DCF returns which, for projects with different lives but constant gross of tax flows, correspond to years to payback.

Table 9·1

Payback periods and DCF returns*

Years to payback required	Life in years 6	8	10	14
3	23½%	27½%	30%	31½%
4	13½%	18%	21%	23%
5	7½%	12%	15%	17½%
6	3½%	8½%	11½%	14%

* The returns shown are the net of corporate tax DCF returns assuming *corporate tax* of 40%, investment allowance of 30%, initial allowance of 10% and reducing balance annual allowance of 20%. This *historic* set of allowances has been used since to date there is no *evidence* of how payback will be applied under the investment grant and imputation tax system.

It is seen from this table that the net of tax rates of return corresponding to different 'years to payback' requirements depend critically on the length of life of the project concerned. With the most common five-year payback standard, the implicit required net of tax rate of return might vary between 7½% and 17½% depending on the life of the project. In contrast with the book rate of return method (discussed in section 2), it is seen that the payback is overwhelmingly biased in favour of short-run projects and, moreover, short-run projects even at very low rates of return as, for example, the 3½% return noted in Table 9.1. It must be concluded, therefore, that in so far as payback is viewed as indicating the financial attractiveness of projects it is an extremely poor approximation, even with the simplifying assumption of uniform gross of tax cash flows.

Perhaps the main objective of the payback approach, however, is as an aid to assessing risk and liquidity. In this context we should first note that these objectives could not be attained by using the *gross of tax* payback concept. Clearly liquidity is related to a company's *net of tax* cash flow and in allowing for risk it is misleading to work in terms of the gross of tax amounts given that there are substantial and virtually certain tax concessions arising in the early years, the very years with which the method is most concerned.

But modified to a net of tax basis the payback concept might be a useful indicator for purposes of risk assessment where the estimated net cash flows from a project are likely to continue for a certain initial period after which they might suddenly cease altogether. Risks of this type do exist in business—the risk that a protective tariff will be completely withdrawn after a time, the risk of a competitor suddenly bringing out a new line which immediately captures nearly the whole market, or the risk of overseas investments suffering uncompensated expropriation by local governments.

But while such risks undoubtedly exist they by no means constitute a large proportion of the commonly encountered business risks. The usual risk in business is not that a project will go on as forecast for a period and then collapse altogether. The risks are rather that a given project will have lower sales, higher costs, unsuspected teething troubles, etc.—in sum the risks that all will not go as well as planned from the very beginning but that the project will probably continue, albeit less profitably than expected. For this type of risk, payback is evidently an unsatisfactory guide to risk appraisal. Since for these projects the main danger is that they will not prove as profitable as expected, the main characteristics to which assessment must be directed are the probabilities and magnitudes of the different possible outcomes, and assessing the extent to which the favourable outcomes offer sufficient potential compensation for the unfavourable.

Nevertheless, payback properly modified to a cash basis and making appropriate allowance for recovering not merely initial capital outlay but also a return on investment, may serve as a useful indicator for risk for those cases in which the primary risk is that of virtually total annihilation at some particular point in time—see Figure 5.1 and reference A 6, section 5.

c. Conclusions

In general, payback as commonly used must be seen as seriously defective both in the objective of reflecting the relative financial attractiveness of projects and as an indicator of use in risk assessment. While it may be modified to serve a useful role in the latter form, there are no practical means by which it could be modified and made useful in the former and critical function of generally reflecting the financial attractiveness of projects. In particular, there are no means by which the method could be used for what we have stressed as the crucial usefulness of the discounting methods of investment appraisal, namely, that of achieving *optimal* rather than merely acceptable investment decisions. This point will be readily appreciated by considering how useful the information about their respective payback periods would be as regards the three following choices (all of which show different capital costs, construction periods and operating lives) for improving an inefficient ferry service: (*a*) a bridge which might last a century or more, (*b*) a road tunnel with a similar life, or (*c*) a modern ferry service, the ships of which would require replacement at say twenty-year intervals. It should be evident that the payback periods would be entirely useless as a basis for discriminating between these three choices.

2. Rate of return[1]

a. Definition

The book rate of return on capital (henceforth referred to as RR) goes under several names of which book rate of return or the accountant's rate of return are the most common. As it has some apparent similarities with the DCF return, it is worth considering in some detail as a possible alternative to the DCF return.

RR is defined as the ratio of profit (net of *accounting* depreciation) to capital. This rate of return is to be compared with some estimate of a company's cost of capital including, where appropriate, some allowance for risk. Net of tax profits can be either initial profits, that is the profits from the first year of operation of a project, or some form of average profits, either an average over the whole life of the project or of only the first five or perhaps ten years of operations. Use of initial profits which could be completely unrepresentative of the profits of later years is manifestly so unsatisfactory that we shall consider only the use of average profits. Finally, capital is defined either as the initial capital outlay on a project including working capital, or less commonly, average capital employed, the average usually being a straight average of capital in the first and last years of a project's life.

[1] Reference A 7, section 1.

b. Shortcomings

i. *Failure to allow for the incidence of capital outlays and earnings*

Consider three simple investment projects, A, B and C, all costing £500 to initiate, having a life of five years, with income arising end-year on average, and the residual value of the assets being zero. Depreciation both for tax purposes and for management accounting purposes is on the straight line basis of £100 a year. Tax is at the rate of 50% and is levied and collected simultaneously at the end of each year. The details of earnings, depreciation, tax and profitability are given in Table 9.2.

Project A has stable profits, Project B rising profits, and Project C falling profits, but all three result in the same *total* profits and thus the same *average* profits. The RR method, based as it is on average profits, would result in all three investments being classified as equal, i.e. as offering a 10% return on initial capital (£50/£500) or a 20% return on 'average' capital (£50/£250). But clearly all three investments are not equally attractive even though their total earnings are the same. Project C's earnings arise earlier than A's which in turn arise earlier than B's. As the differences in annual earnings can be employed elsewhere to advantage (as dividends, loan repayments or investment) in the years before the end of the projects' lives, then C is preferable to A which in turn is preferable to B. This highlights one of the main weaknesses of the RR method compared with discounting methods; it takes no cogniz-ance of the *incidence* of cash flows and so fails to reflect the advantages of near as opposed to distant cash flows. Projects with the same capital cost, life, and total profitability are inevitably ranked equally. Applying discounting methods to the three projects the results are seen to be that C is more profitable than A which in turn is more profitable than B. Further, none of the DCF returns are near either of the two RR variants.

These differences in the three projects would have been even more marked had it been assumed that tax payments were made with a realistic time delay of, say, eighteen months or so, a fact which the RR method, based as it is on an accounting concept of profit as opposed to a cash concept, could not take into account. Even greater differences would have resulted if capital allowances resulted in little or no tax being payable in the early years. This frequently occurs where projects involve heavy investment in plant, particularly in plant which attracts very favourable tax treatment.

Table 9.2

Comparative Profitability assessment

	Years 1	2	3	4	5	Total	Book RR Initial capital	Average capital	DCF return	NPV at 7%
Project A										
Gross earnings	200	200	200	200	200	1,000	10%	20%	15¼%	£115
Less depreciation	-100	-100	-100	-100	-100	-500				
Profits before tax	100	100	100	100	100	500				
Less tax at 50%	-50	-50	-50	-50	-50	-250				
Profits after tax	50	50	50	50	50	250				
Project B										
Gross earnings	100	150	200	250	300	1,000	10%	20%	13½%	£101
Less depreciation	-100	-100	-100	-100	-100	-500				
Profits before tax	—	50	100	150	200	500				
Less tax at 50%	—	-25	-50	-75	-100	-250				
Profits after tax	—	25	50	75	100	250				
Project C										
Gross earnings	300	250	200	150	100	1,000	10%	20%	17½%	£129
Less depreciation	-100	-100	-100	-100	-100	-500				
Profits before tax	200	150	100	50	—	500				
Less tax at 50%	-100	-75	-50	-25	—	-250				
Profits after tax	100	75	50	25	—	250				

Another factor neglected by the RR method is the construction or pre-production period between the commencement of a project and the time when it begins to produce an income. If all the above projects had taken two years before the commencement of earning instead of one year, their 'rates of return' as typically calculated would be unaffected.

ii. *Accuracy of* RR *compared with* DCF

Although the RR method is recognised by some of its adherents as an approximation to more exact methods it is frequently justified on the grounds that it is sufficiently accurate for business purposes. This view turns on some implicit assumption regarding the correct method of calculation and the size of the errors involved in this particular approximation to it. It is our contention that the correct method of calculation involves discounting and so we shall consider the RR as an approximation to the DCF method it most closely resembles.

Consider first the case in which the net cash flows are constant, taxation is zero and the capital assets have negligible resale values at the end of the projects' lives. It is simple to show from its definition that the RR always underestimates the DCF return. The size of the error depends on the size of the DCF return and the life of the project. It is negligible for a project with a life of less than one year or more than, say, fifty, and rises to a peak within these two extremes of project life. The facts are illustrated in Figure 9.1.

In this figure the DCF return is given on the vertical axis against the RR on the horizontal. Each curve gives the relationship between these two rates for capital projects of different lives. Thus the curve marked 'Io years' gives the relationship for an asset with a ten-year life. As the scale of percentages is common to both axes, if the two methods of calculating the rate of return gave the same answer the points would all lie on the dotted 45 degree line. The vertical distances between the curves and this dotted line indicate the errors in the approximations. The two curves for one-year projects and projects with a life of more than fifty years (neither of which is shown separately) lie on the dotted line. The remaining curves are seen here to depart from the 45 degree 'equality' line with decreasing length of life of asset.

The net of tax rates of return within which the majority of capital projects probably fall is 8%-14%. The error in this range as a percentage of the RR is 47% for a ten-year project falling to 26% for a thirty-year project. The size of the error involved in the general case when the

Fig 9·1

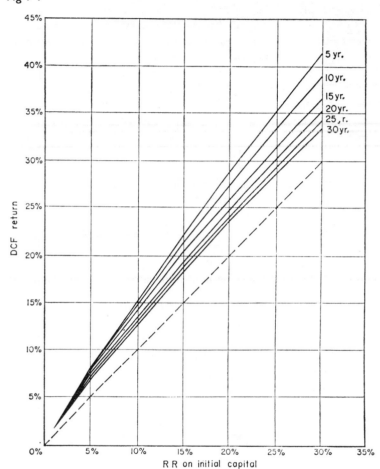

net cash flows are different from year to year cannot be assessed precisely save by a consideration of each individual case.

In general it can be said that the RR and DCF returns come closer where cash flows are increasing over time, and are further apart where cash flows are diminishing over time. This is due to the fact that any changes in the net cash flows in the later years have a far greater effect on the RR compared with the DCF return. In RR calculations a pound received after ten years has precisely the same weight in the calculation as if it were received after one year, while in the DCF return the sums arising in the early years are very much more important. It is found, in fact, that when the DCF return is above 10%, substantial changes in the net cash flows arising after, say, the seventh year have a relatively small influence on the DCF return. This is a point of considerable importance in favour of the DCF return and, of course, the other discounting methods. For while this characteristic follows from the economic logic of the concept, it means that errors of forecasting and uncertainty, which are generally more serious in the later years, are of much less importance than with the RR, because the DCF return results in progressively larger reductions in the present values of the more distant net cash flows.

From this analysis it is apparent *that the RR method strongly discriminates against short term projects (say up to ten years) in favour of long term projects since the absolute error is always larger for the former.* The underestimation is also larger for projects which pay off more heavily in the earlier years than in the later ones (due to favourable capital allowances etc.) and so the method also strongly discriminates against this type of project. The result of these two factors will be to cause companies using the RR to fail to take up some projects of these two types. This is particularly undesirable since such projects are most attractive from the point of view of risk (when of a time nature) and of liquidity. It is a curious feature of the RR that it discriminates strongly against the very type of project which its proponents—who generally favour a conservative concentration on short run returns—are primarily concerned to accept.

So far we have been comparing the RR variant based on *initial* capital with the DCF return. The conclusions for the other RR variant, based on some form of *average* capital are typically the opposite of those so far arrived at. In the case of constant net cash flows, the RR based on average capital employed will typically be double that based on initial capital. As such it will tend significantly to *overestimate* the attractiveness of projects, particularly short-lived ones, or those with large cash flows in the early years. Hence, it will tend to result in companies accepting projects with a prospective yield below the cost of capital.

iii. *Effect of taxation*

A comparison of the net of tax returns given by the RR and DCF methods is shown in Table 9.3. It is seen that the net of tax DCF

Table 9.3

Returns gross and net of tax *

Life of project in years	RR gross of tax	RR net of tax	DCF yield
8	10%	7·0%	16·1%
10	10%	6·6%	15·6%
14	10%	6·1%	14·8%

*The table assumes constant gross of tax cash flows, a 20% grant on all expenditure, free depreciation on plant (80% of total capital cost), 40% initial allowance and 4% annual allowance on buildings. Tax payments and receipt of grant are assumed to occur 12 months after assessment.

returns are typically more than twice the RR net of tax returns even after allowing, when computing the net of tax RR returns, for the 20% cash grants. Moreover, *the net of tax DCF returns* are seen to be half as large[1] again as *the gross of tax RRs*. These large discrepancies arise from the failure of the RR to take into account the *timing* of the capital allowances which make the project's net of tax cash flows exceed its gross of tax cash flows in the critical early years of its life, when, as is typically the case, these allowances can be set against the company's taxable income from other sources.

iv. *Comparability with cost of capital and balance sheet returns*

An important consideration in any method of investment appraisal is that it should produce results which can be meaningfully related to the financial objectives of a company. It is thus desirable that the rate of return found should be measured in the same way and therefore be readily comparable with the rate of return which the company is endeavouring to achieve for its shareholders. The RR also fails in this

[1] The proportionate error of the RRs compared with the DCF returns is fairly constant in these simple examples which assume constant gross cash flows. Where, as is usual, the gross cash flows are irregular, or rising, or there are significant construction periods, then this simple proportionality disappears.

test. These rates of return for shareholders must be gauged by reference to the rate of return which shareholders can be expected to obtain from alternative equity investments (see Chapter 4, section 1). The latter rate of return typically involves a flow of dividends increasing over time followed by a large terminal capital gain as a shareholder realises his equity investment. As the RR cannot satisfactorily measure this pattern of return accruing to shareholders it cannot provide a valid yardstick against which to measure the RRs on a company's investments.

A similar consideration arises where, as a rough guide to the return it is offering shareholders, a company is concerned with its overall rate of return on its equity capital or its capital employed. While neither the RR nor the DCF return is simply and directly related to the rates of return shown in a company's published accounts, the DCF return is more closely related to these accounting rates of return. The reason for this is not far to seek. The RR takes no account of the fact that capital is being reinvested to increase the company's earnings. In sum, a company's *accounts* more nearly reflect the DCF concept of a rate of return on capital outstanding in projects (as opposed to initial undepreciated capital), and for this reason the DCF return generally gives a better approximation to the effect which a project will have on a company's return on capital as shown in its published accounts.

c. Conclusions

The RR must therefore be seen as an extremely unreliable approximation to the DCF return even gross of tax, and an even less reliable approximation to the net of tax DCF return. It is, moreover, biased against short-term projects in the same way that payback is biased against longer term projects, and again, like payback it cannot meaningfully be related to objectives of financial policy in terms of rate of return which companies are seeking to obtain for their shareholders. From this analysis it should be clear that, again like payback, the RR is seriously inadequate for the task of optimising investment decisions.

References

1. NATIONAL ECONOMIC DEVELOPMENT COUNCIL. *Investment in Machine Tools.* H.M.S.O., 1965.
2. R. R. NEILD. *Replacement Policy, National Institute Economic Review,* No. 30, 1965.

10

The Annual Capital Charge (sinking fund) method

The Annual Capital Charge method (or one of its several variants) has been most used in property companies and certain of the nationalised industries, in particular those concerned with large civil engineering schemes, power generation, etc. It has also long been a favoured method of engineers, especially for appraising routine cost saving and replacement investments. The method is most useful in its traditional applications the distinguishing feature of which is the regularity of annual costs and revenues over long periods. Whenever projects have markedly irregular net cash flows or, in the case of replacement decisions whenever obsolescence is the major factor affecting asset life, the method becomes cumbersome, but not impossible, to use and one of the other main discounting methods is usually to be preferred.

As the method is of limited application, this chapter will prove of interest mainly to those engaged in industries commonly using the ACC method. It may, therefore, be omitted by other readers.

I. The basic principle of the annual capital charge method

a. Definition

The ACC method, in common with the other two discounting methods, recognises that there are two costs associated with the use of capital, 'interest' on capital employed and depreciation, or the recovery of capital. To determine whether any investment is profitable, it is necessary to determine whether the net cash flow is sufficient to cover the depreciation and the minimum acceptable 'interest' cost (cost of capital). The NPV method does this by discounting the net cash flows at this minimum 'interest' rate to determine whether the present value of the future net cash flows exceeds the initial cost of the investment. The DCF method involves finding the 'interest' rate which reduces the net cash flow into equality with the initial cost, and then comparing this rate with the cost of capital. If the calculated net present value is sufficiently in excess of initial cost to cover expected risks, or if the DCF return is sufficiently in excess of the minimum cost of capital to cover expected risks, then a project is acceptable.

The ACC method achieves the same result by calculating the average annual capital charge (depreciation plus interest) of a project and comparing this with the project's annual net cash flows (which are assumed to be constant or nearly constant from year to year). If the annual net cash flow exceeds the annual capital charge by a sufficient margin to compensate for expected risks, then the project is acceptable.

To find the ACC of a project it is necessary to know the capital outlay and the life of the project. From this can be calculated the amount of depreciation to be set aside each year which, if invested at the company's cost of capital, will accumulate to the original capital cost of the project. This type of depreciation is known as 'sinking fund' depreciation. It differs from conventional accounting depreciation in that the aggregate annual depreciation provisions are less than the total capital cost, the difference being made up from the 'interest' accumulating on the depreciation fund at the company's cost of capital. This will be clearer when illustrated from the basic example first set out in Table 2.1. Here the project costs £1,000, has a life of three years with annual net cash flows of £388, and the company's cost of capital is 5%.

The problem is to find what regular sum of money invested *end year* at 5% for each year the project is generating income, will grow to £1,000 by the end of the final year of the project's life. This sum is £317. How it was calculated will be shown later: it will first be demonstrated that it is the correct answer.

The £317 at the end of the first year has two full years of investment at 5% compound before the project ends. This sum therefore grows to £317 × 1·05² = £350. The £317 at the end of the second year has only one full year of investment at 5% and so grows to £317 × 1·05 = £333. The £317 at the end of the third year has, of course, no period of investment during which to earn interest, so its value remains unchanged. Thus, by the end of the project's life, the sinking fund of £951 (i.e. £317 × 3) will have grown to £350 + £333 + £317 = £1,000, the initial capital cost of the project. This demonstrates that £317 is the correct annual sum required for the sinking fund depreciation provision.

b. Method of calculation

i. *Basic method*

The value of £317 was calculated from a table of 'compound' factors (the opposite of discount factors). This type of table sets out the amount to which £1 a year, set aside *end year*, will accumulate at different interest rates. An extract from such a table (Table C of reference A) is set out in Table 10.1.

Table 10.1

Extract from Table C of Reference A—the amount to which £1 a year accumulates

Years	Compound factors					
	5%	6%	7%	8%	9%	10%
1	1·00000	1·00000	1·00000	1·00000	1·00000	1·00000
2	2·05000	2·06000	2·07000	2·08000	2·09000	2·10000
3	3·15250	3·18360	3·21490	3·24640	3·27810	3·31000

Thus for the 5% column for year 3, £3·15250 is the amount to which £1 a year arising *end year* will grow at 5% by the *end* of year 3, that is:

$$(£1 \times 1·05^2) + (£1 \times 1·05) + £1 = £3·15250.$$

Using this table it is easy to calculate the annual sinking fund depreciation provision. Thus for three years at 5%, an investment of £1 a year grows to £3·15250. Therefore, the annual sum which will grow to £1,000 over three years at 5% is simply:

$$\frac{£1,000}{3·1525} = £317$$

So much for calculating the depreciation part of the annual capital charge. We turn now to the 'interest' element. This is more easily found, it is simply the interest rate multiplied by the initial capital. In the basic example, this is 5% × £1,000 = £50. Thus the total annual capital charge, interest plus depreciation, is £50 + £317 = £367. As long as the project generates at least this sum for every year of its life, then it should be accepted.

ii. *The annuity method of calculation*

A much easier method of calculating the ACC is to make use of Table B (the present value of £1 a year). The ACC can be found quite simply by dividing the capital invested in a project by the Table B discount factor at the company's cost of capital for the number of years of life of the project. Thus, for the basic example of the project costing £1,000 with a three years' life and a 5% cost of capital, the discount factor from Table B is 2·72325. Dividing the capital cost of £1,000 by 2·72325 gives £367, the same result as calculated by the basic method.

2. Sinking fund method

The sinking fund return (henceforth SFR) is a further development of the ACC. It consists merely of deducting the sinking fund depreciation from the annual net cash flows of a project and expressing the balance as a percentage of the initial capital cost thus giving a rate of return on total capital.

Suppose, for example, that a project has a life of three years, net cash flows of £400 a year, and a capital cost of £1,000. Assuming that the sinking fund rate of interest is 5% it was shown in the previous section that the sinking fund depreciation at 5% interest requires an annual depreciation charge of £317. Hence the balance of the annual net cash flows after deducting this depreciation charge will be £400 – £317 = £83. The sinking fund return is then £83/£1,000 = 8·3%. This return should be compared with a company's cost of capital.

It should be noted that if the sinking fund return comes out at the rate equal to the rate used in the sinking fund then the SFR would equal the DCF return. Thus if the cash flow in the above example had been £367 a year, then the SFR would have been (£367 – £317)/£1,000 = 5%. The DCF return is also 5% as can be ascertained from the fact that the annuity factor (from Table B) for three years is 2·72325 and 2·72325 × £367 = £1,000. For projects with constant cash flows the DCF return will be less than the SFR if the sinking fund interest rate is less than the DCF return, and higher if the DCF return is less than the sinking fund interest rate.

3. Some practical difficulties

The above ways of calculating the ACC need some further elaboration to cover cases in which the capital expenditures on a project occur over a period, or where cash flows arise at other than yearly intervals.

a. Multi-period capital outlays

When capital outlays occur over more than one discounting period, a commonly used rule is to accumulate the separate capital outlays with interest at the cost of capital to the time of the last capital outlay before the net cash flows begin, and to treat that sum as if it were a single capital outlay at that date. Consider an example in which the capital outlays and net cash flows are as follows:

Years	0	1	2	3-9 inclusive
Cash flows	$-£341$	$-£800$	$-£300$	$£300$

Assuming for this example a capital cost of 8% the equivalent capital sum invested at the end of year 2 is:

$$(£341 \times 1\cdot08^2) + (£800 \times 1\cdot08) + £300$$
$$= £398 + £864 + £300 = £1,562$$

The project would then be treated as if it were a seven-year project costing £1,562 and giving rise to £300 a year. Its ACC at 8% is then £1,562 divided by the seven year 8% discount factor from Table B, $£1,562 \div 5\cdot20637 = £300$, thus indicating that the net cash flows only just equal the ACC and that the project is marginal.

b. Cash flows arising other than end year

A further difficulty arises when the gap between the capital outlays and the start of the cash income is not one year (or a multiple of a year) but some different period. Suppose a capital outlay of £9,615 gives rise to £3,880 eighteen months later plus two further sums of £3,880 at twelve-month intervals thereafter. To find the ACC in this case it is merely necessary to calculate half a year's 'interest' on the capital outlay at the appropriate cost of capital. This reduces the calculation of the ACC to the conventional case where the capital outlay is only a year away from the net cash flow stream. Taking an 8% cost of capital, and halving this to give the half year rate, the equivalent capital outlay six months later is simply $£9,615 \times 1\cdot04 = £10,000$. The ACC is then found in the normal way.

11

The discounting methods compared

This chapter considers the relative merits of the three main discounting methods. Correctly used all three methods are numerically correct and would lead to the same investment decisions. The choice between the methods must therefore be made on operational grounds. Our conclusion is that on these grounds—specifically convenience in aiding the evaluation of projects under conditions of uncertainty and economy of presentation —the DCF is generally preferable in the majority of applications.

1. DCF versus NPV

The DCF and NPV methods must be compared on both technical and operational grounds. The main conclusion from this comparison is that for the majority of capital project appraisals the DCF method has decisive operational advantages over the NPV method, although some modifications are occasionally required. But for certain technical problems such as analysing all the possible ways of undertaking a major investment (certainly in the early stages of an optimisation evaluation), and for certain specialised tasks such as valuing a company for takeover purposes, the NPV method has certain distinct advantages. In short the two methods are essentially complementary and both will be found generally useful.

a. A technical comparison of NPV and DCF

i. *Determining acceptable projects*
The DCF and NPV methods will both result in the same division of projects into those which are acceptable and those which should be rejected when a company has a constant cost of capital. The reason for this is fairly obvious; projects with a DCF in excess of the company's

cost of capital will also have a positive NPV at this rate of discount. Hence, accepting all projects with a DCF return in excess of the cost of capital or accepting all projects with a positive NPV at the cost of capital must lead to the same selection of projects.

ii. *Mutually exclusive projects and the incremental cash flow approach*

Mutually exclusive projects are defined as those which compete for acceptance in that it is probably not possible or desirable for a company to accept more than one. They are of fairly common occurrence. Typical examples are alternative types of plant for the same basic process or two or more plans for the use of one plot of land. Another example is two or more financially acceptable projects when a company has sufficient management staff or labour for only one. In all such cases a choice must be made between two or more possibilities.

It should be clear on reflection that the simple DCF returns cannot usually be used to discriminate satisfactorily between such competing choices because the DCF return (like other rates of return) does not give any indication of either the *amount* of capital involved in an investment or the *duration* of the investment. Consider the simple example set out in Table 11.1 below, where a choice must be made between the mutually exclusive projects A and B, where the company's cost of capital is 8%.

Table 11.1

Project	Capital cost	Annual cash flow	Life	NPV at 8%	DCF return
	£	£		£	
A	502,000	100,000	10 years	169,000	15%
B	780,000	144,000	10 years	186,000	13%
B-A	278,000	44,000	10 years	17,000	9·6%

In this simple example the two projects A and B have the same life but involve substantially different amounts of capital. Because the DCF returns of 15% and 13% take no explicit account of this fact, these returns cannot be used to discriminate between A and B. Discrimination can easily be made, however, on the basis of the *incremental* cash flows as indicated in the bottom line in the table marked 'B-A'. This line shows the additional £278,000 of capital invested in B and the additional or incremental annual cash flow of £44,000 arising from it. This incremental project has a 9·6% return. Thus we may describe project B as having everything that is offered by project A plus £278,000 extra invested to give £44,000 a year for ten years, which gives a DCF return of 9·6% and an NPV of £17,000. *Providing both projects A and B would be acceptable on their own,*[1] the choice between them can be made by considering the incremental return on B-A or the incremental NPV, depending on the management's preference between the two approaches. Incremental capital investments frequently are subject to significantly higher degrees of risk—as, for example, when the project with the higher capital cost involves a new and more capital intensive process, or involves securing a substantially higher sales volume than a competing project. Because of this it is always worth evaluating incremental investments separately whatever method of analysis is used and even when the higher cost project also has the higher DCF return.

Where a choice must be made between many possibilities and not just two or three, the work of comparison may well prove tedious using the incremental DCF approach rather than the NPV approach. Where the DCF approach is the preferred method, this handicap can be overcome by using NPV to narrow the choice down to only two or three, then the incremental DCF approach can be used for the final selection and presentation.

A final practical point of some importance is that in dealing with mutually exclusive projects, either by DCF or NPV, it is essential to choose an equal life for the competing projects being considered. Thus if in the example shown in Table 11.1, Project A had had a life of only five years to Project B's ten years, we should have needed to consider the action which the company would have taken at the end of the five years after Project A had finished. If this had involved further capital expenditures and outlays over the following five years, then these should be explicitly stated and would have to be taken into account when computing the incremental cash flows.

iii. *Ranking*

A fairly common theoretical objection to the use of the DCF method is that it does not rank investment projects in their true order of attractiveness. The true order of attractiveness in this context is taken to be that dictated by net present values. This is essentially another version of the argument regarding mutually exclusive projects in which Project A seems preferable to Project B on the basis of their DCF returns while

---

[1] Before choosing between the projects it must first be determined whether or not either would be acceptable on its own. Most managements would want to know the separate DCF returns of both projects to take this decision.

on the NPV basis B seems preferable to A. But the NPV ranking order is significant only in the absence of risk. Where projects are subject to risk, particularly different degrees of risk, their order of attractiveness can, as demonstrated above, differ from that given by their estimated NPVs. More important than this is the fact that in the normal investment choice the ranking order of all investments is totally irrelevant. Providing a company has a sufficient supply of funds at its estimated cost of capital it merely has to decide whether the prospective projects have a sufficient return above this cost of capital to compensate for the risks involved, and so qualify for acceptance. It matters not at all whether a project is ranked first, third or tenth, so long as it qualifies for acceptance—the overall ranking order is of no practical interest or importance. Where a company has insufficient funds at its disposal to accept all profitable prospective projects, however, then it is in a capital rationing situation. This can pose a difficult selection problem but the simple NPV ranking order is also irrelevant to its solution. The capital rationing problem and its solution, is briefly discussed in section 1b of the next chapter.

iv. *Reinvestment assumption*

A common misconception regarding DCF returns is that they imply that the capital recovered from a project is reinvested at the project's DCF rate of return over the remainder of its life. This misconception arises from misunderstanding the definition of a DCF return (see section 2a of Chapter 2). The DCF return is correctly defined as the rate of return on the capital outstanding in a project during every year of its life. This interpretation no more assumes reinvestment at the project's rate of return than the statement that a bank is receiving a 6% rate of interest on an overdraft implies that the bank is reinvesting repayments of the overdraft at 6%.

v. *Situation in which the DCF is meaningless*

In certain easily recognised though rarely encountered situations it is possible for an investment project to have two or more DCF returns, and such returns are meaningless. This difficulty typically arises when projects have inescapable large cash outflows towards the end of their lives, a characteristic of very few capital projects. Where such situations arise, a company is effectively in the position of lending (or investing) money at the DCF rate of return over part of the life of the project, and then in the latter part of the life reversing its role and becoming a borrower at the DCF rate of return. While it is obviously attractive to lend or invest at high rates of return it is correspondingly unattractive to borrow at high rates of return, hence, a return which relates to a combination of these two situations must be meaningless.

This meaningless DCF will arise if, discounting the company's cost of capital, all the cash flows from *any* time onwards in the project's life give a negative present value. For this to occur the negative cash flows typically have to be heavy and occur towards the end of the project's life and such situations are very uncommon. (The relatively small negative cash flow due to tax payments occurring at the end of the life of most projects is too small to be of any numerical significance.) The problem of meaningless DCFs in practice is therefore very rare and for those situations in which it does occur reference A5 provides a relatively simple method of overcoming the difficulty by giving a more general definition of the DCF return. (The problem arises more commonly in complex technical applications of discounting—see Chapter 7, section 2.)

b. An operational comparison of NPV and DCF

From the comparison of the DCF and NPV methods given in the previous section it will be appreciated that properly used both methods are equally sound technically. The choice between them must therefore be made on the basis of operational advantage. It is our own opinion and experience that in this respect the DCF is decisively the superior method. This superiority is particularly marked in the context of assessing the return offered for risk bearing because the DCF measures profitability as a return per unit of capital per unit of time it is invested (that is, exposed to risk). It is therefore measuring profitability in the same dimensions of quantity and time as risk, since risk generally depends on the amount of capital exposed to risk over time. (There may, of course, be other risks—e.g. risk of capital overruns—but these can be allowed for separately by evaluating the DCF returns on the different possible capital costs.) Thus the difference between the DCF return and the cost of capital provides a ready indicator of the return being offered for risk bearing in the relevant dimensions of the main risks involved. NPV, which takes the form of an absolute quantity of money, lacks this very important advantage. While in the absence of risk there would be little to choose between the DCF and NPV methods, the presence of risk makes the DCF method the more useful of the two. It is primarily for this reason that the DCF method is more readily accepted by businessmen (particularly senior managers) than the NPV method.

In part this preference arises from the tendency of businessmen to think of profitability in terms of percentage rates in many other contexts, e.g. sales margins, but this general preference for a rate of return approach should not be dismissed as mere lack of sophistication. It is commonly observed in many complex situations that factors are expressed in terms of percentages and rates per unit of time, in order to establish relationships between the relevant variables. The change in national output, for example, is expressed as a percentage rate for a unit of time rather than as an absolute sum of money.

The difficulty of using the NPV method for investment evaluation under conditions of uncertainty is precisely the difficulty of relating it numerically to the obviously important factors of the amount of capital at risk and the period of risk. It is clearly incorrect to re-express a Net Present Value as a percentage of capital cost averaged out over a project's life—this would be merely a crude version of the DCF return. (It would also suffer from the same difficulty concerning a project's life as the ACC method discussed in section 2b below.) But under conditions of uncertainty it is usually imperative to establish a meaningful relationship between the amount of capital at risk, the period the capital is at risk, and the prospective profitability. It is because the DCF method more adequately meets this requirement than the NPV that the DCF method has the decisive operational advantage under conditions of uncertainty.

The second major operational advantage of DCF is in its economy of presentation. Given the very considerable opportunity cost of senior management time, this advantage is extremely valuable. The particular advantage of DCF in this respect is its economy in indicating the area of disagreement among top management as regards the acceptability of different projects. Inevitably there will be disagreement at senior level regarding the appropriate level of return for investments of differing degrees of risk. If the net present value approach were to be used, a whole series of net present values at different rates of discount would need to be presented in order to meet the requirements of the various senior executives concerned in evaluating the investment. This could lead to a considerable proliferation of data. In contrast, the provision of the DCF return enables senior management to perceive immediately whether or not the DCF is sufficiently above the various desired rates of discount considered appropriate for a particular category of investment.

While strongly arguing in favour of the DCF method on operational grounds, we also accept that the NPV method has certain advantages in specific cases—as, for example, in discriminating between a large number of mutually exclusive projects, particularly in the early stages of project analysis, and for certain specialised investment projects such as takeovers. In short, the DCF method should be the primary method of investment appraisal, with the NPV method playing a useful but subsidiary role.

2. Annual Capital Charge and sinking fund return[1]

a. Conceptual differences: SFR and DCF

As illustrated in section 2 of Chapter 10, the SFR method and the DCF method give identical returns only where the sinking fund is assumed to accumulate at the DCF rate. Since this could only arise by chance (given that projects must vary substantially in their DCF returns) it is evidently only by chance that these two methods will give identical returns. The SFR, although giving a rate of return, must therefore be seen as a method based on a quite different concept from that of DCF. The SFR concept is that of the rate of return earned by *all* the capital originally invested over the whole life of the project where any recovery of such capital is presumed to be reinvested in capital projects offering a marginal rate of return equal to the company's cost of capital. In this sense it is a return on the total capital originally invested where this return results from an amalgam of capital projects, namely the initial investment project and the series of marginal rate of return projects in which all capital recoveries are invested until the end of the life of the initial project.

b. Problem of project life and sinking fund rate

The usefulness of both ACC and SFR turns first on the extent to which the project has a clearly defined life and secondly on the validity of the assumed rate of return on the sinking fund depreciation provisions. A project has a poorly defined life—for the purposes of this rate of return —if, for example, over a substantial part of its life earnings are declining appreciably so that this part of its life is economically unimportant to the project. In this instance it may be that the annual net cash flow would be insufficient in the later years of the project's life to cover the

[1] Reference A 5, section 3.

annual capital charge so that, even by this standard, most of the capital will have been recovered and most of the profit earned in the earlier part of the project's life. Under these conditions it would evidently be economically confusing to reduce what may have been an originally high return on the initial investment by effectively averaging it with a long period of marginal investments through the presumed working of the sinking fund over this later and economically unimportant phase of the initial project's life. Similar difficulties arise where a project involves a series of capital outlays over a long construction period.

The second consideration determining the general usefulness of the ACC and SFR is the rate of return at which the project's depreciation provisions are deemed to be reinvested. This sinking fund rate to be meaningful must be based on a factual assessment of the actual use to which cash generated by the project will be put and this must be seen in terms of the *marginal* changes to a company's capital investment programme or financing. For example, property companies engaging in investments which are substantially financed by debt capital may be using cash generated by their existing property investments to 'back out' further borrowing, or alternatively to invest in further property investments offering much the same return as the interest rate on borrowing. A sinking fund based on this interest rate may generally be appropriate. For an ordinary company drawing capital from a diversity of sources, however, the sinking fund rate of return would need to be at its net of tax cost of capital as described in Chapter 4.

c. Evaluation of the ACC and SFR

It is technically possible to use the ACC or SFR methods to provide the correct answer to any investment problem. In many cases, however, their application would be extremely clumsy—as, for example, where the projects have irregular cash flows. In the latter case—which will arise in almost all situations involving capital allowances—it is necessary as a first step in the analysis to smooth out the cash flows by reducing them to their present value and then dividing by an annuity factor to convert this present value into a constant annual sum over the life of the asset. As noted above, this involves the further difficulty of determining the life of the asset, and this may be difficult where long construction periods are involved or where earnings are declining towards the end of the life of the project. Essentially then the method is technically correct but this is merely because in the form that is required for realistic capital budgeting it is no more than the net present value turned into an equivalent constant annual sum.

The case for these two methods is, however, sometimes based on misconceptions as to the theoretical basis of the alternative methods— as, for example, a belief that DCF implies that the capital recovered from the project is reinvested at the same rate of return as in the initial project itself. As is pointed out in section 1a above, this view is entirely erroneous.

The real case for these methods must rest on their clarity of conception and their administrative convenience. In our view DCF is preferable on both counts. As regards clarity of conception, it avoids the difficulty of having to specify an exact life in which each year counts equally (as it does in the ACC/SFR methods), it isolates the single project being considered by avoiding the troublesome concept of a sinking fund, and it provides a rate of return which is most relevant in evaluating the compensation being offered for risk bearing. On the administrative convenience of the DCF method we have already commented (see section 1b above). By its nature, however, this general conclusion can be no more than an expression of informed opinion. A contrary opinion is given in reference 1.

3. Discounting, profits and share prices

a. The problem of incorrect share valuations[1]

It is generally the case that the price of a company's shares as they are traded on the Stock Exchange does not, in the view of the management, correctly reflect the true value of those shares in the light of the management's expectations of future cash flows which will be generated by the company's business, taking into account the Stock Market's valuation of similar companies in apparently similar situations. Fairly frequently the shares will appear undervalued, particularly in the case of a fairly new company or one with considerable but still embryonic growth prospects; sometimes the shares will seem overvalued, if the market expects continuation of a growth or level of earnings which can no longer be sustained. In the case of the former, the cost of newly-raised capital to the company will be

[1] This section summarises a very technical and difficult subject analysed in great depth in Reference A Chapter 9, to which readers should refer for answers to specific questions.

abnormally high, and 'new' shareholders—that is, shareholders requiring shares by issue or by market purchase—will gain at the expense of 'old' shareholders. In the case of the latter, the cost of capital may be too low, and either the company may make unwise investment decisions on the strength of it, or new shareholders may acquire shares which, on their failure to yield the expected return, are sold in sufficiently large quantities to set up a volatile movement in the company's share price.

Generally such under- or over-evaluations are short-lived (up to 1 year) and of comparatively small magnitude—say within 15% of the level which the company's management believes to be correct. But when the incorrect market valuation persists at levels further removed from the true value than this, managements owe their shareholders and themselves the responsibility of endeavouring to correct the fault. The most obvious way is to publish, as best as can be done, the same information about prospective earnings and cash flows as the management has, so that on reflection the market can establish a more soundly-based view of the company. This process should include publicising the management's investment criteria and expectations.

If values still remain significantly out of line, the management should repeat as an extraordinary exercise what should in any case be a regular one, the internal valuation of their shares. This should consist of the most realistic forecast possible of the equity cash flows of the company as far as can be reasonably foreseen—say 5-10 years ahead—together with the trend for the next 10-15 years thereafter. Discounting these at the company's equity cost of capital, including any surplus realisable assets, should produce the company's present total equity value. In order to test the severity of the market value divergence, reasonable variations to the main assumptions should be tested to see how wide a possible range of values could be sensible.

This exercise should be accompanied by consultation with the company's financial advisers to ensure that the management is not at fault in its view of the market's valuation of similarly placed companies. (It is often the case that an apparent undervaluation applies, for reasons of fashion, ignorance, or so on, to a complete industry sector.)

If after all this the management is still convinced that its shares are incorrectly valued, it should take especial care that any capital investment decisions made during the state of faulty valuation are thoroughly and properly analysed. Since the difficulty lies chiefly with the cases where the shares are undervalued, the following discussion relates chiefly to that situation.

b. Faulty valuation of the whole market

In general there is no real problem if it has been decided by the management and its advisers that the faulty valuation in fact applies as well to the general level of share prices. Provided that the company is financing its proposed equity investment either from internal retained earnings or from rights issues—that is, new capital raised from its existing shareholders—the management should only regard the market aberration as a reason for deferring investment if it can be sure that postponement would increase the *present* value of the investment whatever the movement in the meantime of share prices. (In this instance the company's normal cost of capital should be used for evaluation purposes, regardless of the apparent cost of capital at the time of the faulty valuation.) It is worth noting why this applies in the case of rights issues. Had the company not made its rights issue because of the market state, the existing shareholders could otherwise have invested in other companies and seen these new investments rise or fall with the market. Provided their normal return on capital is achieved on the investment made by the company financed by the rights issue, they should achieve the same result by taking up their rights and foregoing this opportunity of investing elsewhere in the market.

In the rare case of an investment by a company which requires cash from new shareholders—for example, an acquisition which involves the issue of shares—when the market as a whole is unreasonably depressed, it is less likely that immediate investment can be justified, since, by waiting until the market has recovered and with it the company's own shares, fewer new shares will have to be issued, resulting in a reduced dilution. The converse, of course, holds true when the market is over-valued except insofar as the company incurs obligations to the new shareholders.

c. Undervaluation of the company's shares

When the management of a company finds its own shares chronically and significantly undervalued relative both to their 'true' value and to the market as a whole—for example, during a recession in that company's major line of business, or because of a long gestation period for a big new project—the question of new investments requires even more careful handling. Nevertheless, where there is no question of having to raise new equity capital during the period of undervaluation—which, though prediction might be difficult, cannot be more than temporary—then the company is safe to continue to use its normal equity cost of capital when considering the investment of retained earnings, since this will reflect simply the return the shareholders could obtain by investing elsewhere. It is only when the company has to issue new shares, which may cause changes in the proportionate holdings of its existing shareholders at a time when their future earnings prospects are temporarily undervalued, that the underevaluation becomes a problem.

The general answer is clear from the preceding comments in this section, that where it is clear that any change is going to be made to existing shareholders' proportionate interest in the company's future earnings, the finance-raising, and hence the proposed investment, should be postponed. This will be found to be the case in virtually all circumstances and irrespective of whether the eventual investment when accepted in the future is financed by retained earnings or by the new issue contemplated now: the project should be postponed only until such time as either retained earnings are sufficient to finance it, obviating new capital raising, or the undervaluation has been largely corrected, permitting the new capital to be raised without risk of it being held by 'new' shareholders who will disproportionately dilute the interests of the 'old' shareholders in the future earnings of the existing business. In analysis of specific proposals it will be necessary to quantify the difference between, on the one hand, the return to the existing shareholders from their existing undiluted expectations and that from the postponed new investment, and, on the other hand, their diluted return from the existing activities and the return from the new project taken up immediately by means of new capital issues. In nearly all cases where the current undervaluation is at all marked it will be found that this difference is so great that it constitutes an impossible hurdle for the project to cross.

d. The relationship of discounting and profits

The charge is sometimes laid against discounting methods of investment appraisal that they fail to take into account the importance to the stock market of reported book profits. The circumstances in which this criticism is generally made are those where a high DCF return is found, although book profits in the early years are low, and the critics generally advocate adopting a lower DCF standard with emphasis transferred to projects which provide early and smoothly growing book profits.

These circumstances can be seen to be similar to those in which there might be undervaluation of the company's shares, the approach to which has been indicated above. It can also arise where the depreciation rules adopted in the published accounts provide for very heavy early depreciation charges. However, this is probably entirely within the company's control, and it would clearly be incorrect to regard as a serious flaw in a project something which results from the adoption of a particular accounting method. Cases where there is a genuine risk of share undervaluation caused by a project's impact on early profit are not too common, and are generally related to major acquisitions and to major projects with long construction periods. In these cases it is obviously sensible to examine carefully the effect on profits, but it would be exceptional to feel that a project which passed the DCF standard should be rejected because of its profits effect. What is vital is that the DCF *standard* should not be lowered for the sake of obtaining smooth growth of profits; this can only result in the misallocation of resources and in the attainment of less than optional returns on the shareholders' funds. Good investment evaluation certainly requires more than the discounting of cash flows, but it never requires less.

This subject is discussed in Reference A, Chapter 9, Section 9.

Reference

1. PEARSON HUNT, *Financial Analysis in Capital Budgeting*, Graduate School of Business Administration, Boston, 1964.

12

Special problems: optimal financing, expansion, etc.

It is not possible in a short book to discuss the many special complexities which arise in practice in the appraisal of capital projects. In this chapter, therefore, the more important special problems are briefly considered and the sources of further information are indicated. The problems fall into two categories, those which relate to optimal financing policies in different conditions, and those which relate to certain complex types of project.

I. Optimal financing

a. Financing and distribution policy[1]

In Chapter 4 the likely cost of capital for a typical public company was considered. Three main categories of finance were distinguished apart from virtually automatic sources such as creditors; first, short and long term loans; second, equity capital from retained earnings; third, equity capital from new issues. As was shown in Table 4.1, there is little effective difference in the cost of retained earnings and new issues, but fixed interest capital is considerably cheaper (4·5% compared with 11·3%).

Given these facts, the optimal financing policy (that which maximises the benefits to shareholders) will generally be to raise the maximum long and short term debt consistent with maintaining the standing or reputation of a company's equity shares. More formally, it is to raise the amount of debt which maximises the total market value of a company's equity plus debt capital.

[1] Reference A 15 and reference 1.

In the case of short-term debt, banks and finance houses will usually restrict their lending so that the ratio of current assets to current liabilities[1] (where the latter term includes all short-term loans) should not normally be less than 2 to 1, with $1\frac{1}{2}$ to 1 as the probable minimum. The optimal rule then is to borrow the maximum short-term funds possible within these institutional restraints.

Similar institutional requirements tend to restrict the amount of long-term debt that may be borrowed to around 25%-30% of total tangible assets less current liabilities, providing the net cash flow is adequate to cover interest and loan repayments usually by a factor of four or five. Occasionally, where assets are deemed to be at less than normal risk, a higher debt percentage is possible, e.g. in property companies. Optimal financing then requires a company to borrow up to the appropriate conventional limit of net tangible assets. It is the case with many British companies that their debt percentages are usually less than half the possible amount because of misplaced financial conservatism. Such companies are using equity funds in place of debt funds and consequently need to look for a much higher return on investment.

Having established the optimal balance of debt and equity capital a company should then seek to establish the optimal balance between the two sources of equity capital, retained earnings and new share issues. This essentially involves increasing the proportion of earnings retained (subject of course to the cut-off rates established in Chapter 4) until the marginal cost of such retentions rises to the cost of externally raised equity capital. (High levels of retentions will generally cause shareholders to require higher rates of return on the extra retentions—see reference 2—and this will accordingly tend to increase the return which a company needs to obtain on its retained earnings; that is, the cost of retained earnings will increase.)

b. Capital rationing[2]

Capital rationing arises in a company whenever it has more investment opportunities than available funds. In large companies this commonly arises under conditions of severe competition which seriously reduce profits perhaps at a time when heavy 'defensive' investment is needed. In such a situation of low profit it may be extremely expensive to raise further equity funds, and the same is likely to be true of debt capital. In any case, as was argued in the previous section, there are

[1] See Appendix A, Basic accounting principles.
[2] Reference A 4, Section 7.

clearly defined limits to the amount of debt capital available to any company. In small companies capital rationing sometimes arises because many such companies do not yet have full access to the capital market; they are too small or their profit record is not yet good enough. Another frequent cause is that the boards of many small companies are unwilling to borrow money because of their dislike of restrictive conditions imposed by lenders. Similarly, they are unwilling to raise more equity capital for fear of losing control of their company. Others just prefer to grow at the pace they can finance from internally generated funds. Whatever the cause, capital rationing renders unsatisfactory the assumption that a company has a cost of capital equal to that of externally raised capital and project evaluation must be modified to take this into account.

In the long-term capital rationing situation, the company needs to determine the opportunity cost of capital. If this can be assumed roughly constant year by year, it can be defined as the rate of return (the cut-off rate) which will exclude sufficient projects so as to bring the demand for capital for investment into equality with the available capital. The DCF returns are then compared with this opportunity cost net of tax.

The problem is somewhat more complicated where the company is only temporarily in this capital rationing position—for example, where there are exceptionally heavy short term demands for funds or where it is temporarily difficult for the company to get all the capital it requires.

The method of attack in this case basically is that of setting the required discount rate at a higher level *for the period of capital shortage*. The rate should be raised to the point at which it will reduce the demand for capital in the company to that available over this period. For example, a company experiencing a period of capital rationing which is expected to last three years might try discounting projects, to determine the DCF return, at a 4% higher discount rate over the first three years of capital rationing than for the remaining years. Consider the case of a capital project costing £33,300 and giving rise to net cash flows of £10,000 for five years. The DCF return where the company is looking for an additional 4% return over the period of capital shortage might be computed as follows. A trial rate should be chosen for the last two years of the project's life. If this is 12% then the first three years should be discounted at 12% + 4% = 16%, and the remaining two years at 12%. The present value of the cash flows with this discounting is:

$$\frac{£10,000}{(1\cdot16)} + \frac{£10,000}{(1\cdot16)^2} + \frac{£10,000}{(1\cdot16)^3} + \frac{£10,000}{(1\cdot16)^3(1\cdot12)} + \frac{£10,000}{(1\cdot16)^3(1\cdot12)^2} = £33,286$$

As the capital cost is £33,300 this discounting makes the net present value approximately zero. (If the net present value had been negative in this example it would have been necessary to try a lower trial rate for the long term, say 11%. This would require that the first three years be discounted at 11% + 4% = 15%, and the last two years at 11%.) Hence the DCF return is 16% over the first three years and 12% thereafter. This has precisely the same interpretation as, say, obtaining 16% interest on the capital outstanding on a bank overdraft for three years and then obtaining 12% on the capital outstanding in the last two years.

The 4% additional return over the first three years would need to be determined by general trial and error applied to all the marginal items in the company's capital budget. But at the final stage of the capital budgeting analysis it should not be too difficult to try a succession of higher rates to determine the rate which is required to bring the demand for capital into equilibrium with the supply.

c. Cash surplus[1]

It is fairly common for large companies to experience periods when internally generated funds substantially exceed investment opportunities, a condition known as cash surplus. Such companies may be optimally financed with high debt gearing during their numerous expansion periods but the growing cash surplus seems to make it pointless to raise any further debts. The 'obvious' solution in these circumstances is to pay out more profits in dividends, and if this still fails to eliminate the surplus to consider the many possible ways of returning such funds to shareholders. Where, for whatever reasons, these policies are not followed, the company clearly should not continue to apply its old cost of capital standards since if it does the cash surplus will continue and may even increase.

The company should first consider its portfolio investment policy. Most company portfolio investment is placed in short-dated gilt-edged securities or similar fixed interest securities. This is a reasonable procedure where the surplus is likely to last only two or three years after which it will be absorbed in profitable investments. But where such cash is not required for three years or more then the company should consider investment in the equity of other companies. (No significant tax

[1] Reference A 16.

disadvantages arise from such investment as long as the investing company's own dividends exceed its dividend income.) Although this policy involves risks the company's shareholders may reasonably be presumed to prefer the normal risks and higher prospective returns of equity investment to the security and the low *real* returns, commonly 1% or less, which are available on fixed interest investment.

If this policy is unacceptable then, however regrettable this may be from the viewpoint of the company's shareholders, the second best alternative must be to follow through the logic of the situation and lower the required return on investments. The company should consider what rate of return shareholders would be prepared to accept on investments of normal commercial risk if the only alternative open to them is in fact investment through the company in fixed interest securities. For example, if fixed interest securities are offering, say, $6\frac{1}{2}\%$ the shareholders might be considered prepared to accept, say, 9% on normal commercial risk investment and only this $6\frac{1}{2}\%$ on virtually risk-free investment.

2. Projects requiring special analysis

There are certain types of project which are commonly identifiable not only by the frequency with which they occur but also by the fact that they contain certain similarities in every occurrence, an understanding of which can greatly assist in the systematic and thorough analysis of them. One such project is that of the evaluation of companies for merger or acquisition; the complexities and importance of this are, however, so considerable that the whole of Chapter 8 was devoted to their discussion. The remainder of the present Chapter contains consideration of four other frequently occurring types of problems, which are in turn discussed in depth in Reference A 11.

a. Analysis of expansion opportunities[1]

The analysis of expansion possibilities will be found to be fairly straightforward, as indeed is the evaluation of most investment opportunities once the full interdependence of all the factors is understood. The common features of most expansion problems are, however, worthy of description since familiarity will then ease the task of considering what is probably the most common type of investment project.

[1] Reference A 11.

(i) *The market*

The possibility of expansion might arise either because of the belief in the possibility of obtaining a greater market share or because of a growing total market in which mere maintenance of an existing share requires expansion. Because, however, expansion increases the resources committed, the care with which the market situation is considered must be at least as great as that with which it would be analysed in the case of an entirely new venture. If an existing market share is to be expanded, attention should be paid to the likely reaction of competitors, and detailed analysis should be made of any contractual or long-term relationships they have with customers and of their ability to enter severe price competition where they should, with their capacity already installed, be in a good position to beat a new investment. This will in turn require an examination of the sensitivity of demand to price reductions or to other forms of competitive promotion which might be adopted in defence of existing market shares. The additional marketing costs of achieving the deeper penetration will require assessment, as will the effect of the planned marketing strategy on one's own existing market share and product prices.

If, on the other hand, the expansion results from a total market growth, it will be necessary to examine the reasons for, and the likely duration of, the increased demand. In this case the possibility of competitive action from alternative means of satisfying the market—different materials, different types of sales outlets, imports—should be assessed. Once again extra marketing effort must be costed, and the possibility of responding to market growth by changing to greater margin business rather than to greater volume must be carefully evaluated, with the market's sensitivity to price increases being the key element.

(ii) *Operating costs*

One of the benefits of expanding business is that, just as some capital costs can be shared with the existing business, thereby realising some of the economies of scale, so there might be certain operating costs which are not dependent on volume and which will similarly permit operating economies to be achieved. Knowledge of the pattern of fixed and variable costs of the existing business will be very useful in estimating the operating expenses of the expansion, but care should be taken to see differences between the methods of operation which might cause different cost structures. An obvious possibility here lies in the costs of overtime or of shift working, where the entire expansion might be made possible by greater utilisation of existing capacity. Careful analysis of operating costs and practice often reveals considerable potential for capacity increases, even if operating costs rise as a result, and these can be evaluated in comparison with capital investment costs.

One vital area of operating expenditure to consider in the field of expansion projects is that of management. All too often the expansion of a successful business causes strains on management which result in the deterioration of the entire enterprise. This is one of the most difficult areas to judge in advance, since any successful manager believes himself to be capable of managing larger enterprises than his current responsibility. Where the expansion under review is of any significance by comparison with the existing operation, the question of managerial ability is often best resolved with outside advice.

(iii) *Capital costs and financing*

Where the expansion requires augmentation of facilities on an existing site, the limitations of that location will have to be thoroughly explored. Will an increase in capacity be totally independent of existing productive equipment, or will it in some areas share plant already used? If the latter, will the added throughput at these stages require changes to established process flows? Is the whole site equipped with adequate infrastructure to support increased production—car parks, access for supplies and despatches, power, water and drains will all require investigation. These all appear to be obvious points, but they are often forgotten in the context of the addition of capacity to a successful and familiar operation already in existence.

Having considered the areas outlined above, the analyst can derive the additional costs and revenues engendered by the proposed expansion. Because it consists to a greater or lesser extent, of an addition to an existing enterprise, there will be some costs or revenues which are in some respect common both to the existing and to the new part of the operation. To determine the economic viability of the expansion it is both impracticable and incorrect to attempt to apportion these shared items between the two elements of the new total operation. The evaluation should rather be conducted on an 'incremental' basis. In this, the cash flows of the new total business after expansion should be determined. From these should be deducted the cash flows of the existing business, which should be forecast as easily; the result will give the cash flows of the increment to be provided by the expansion the return on which is then simply calculable. Obviously a number of different assumptions will have to be tested by means of sensitivity analysis, but the basic method will remain the same.

One question which will frequently recur is that of the timing and size of steps in what is planned as a continuous expansion programme. Where fairly constant additions to capacity seem to be justified by market expectations, the analyst will in nearly all cases be faced with a large number of different ways of adding the increments: he will have to compare the costs of a succession of small increments with those of fewer larger steps, looking not only at the capacity of the process as a whole but at the capacities of each individual production unit, since some units will only be capable of large increments while others are highly flexible. The simplest way of comparing these will be to determine the *total* costs of producing the planned output over the period of time in question—10 years, say—by the various means and comparing the present values of the various streams. The optimum route should then be apparent.

At the same time as analysing the costs of expanding existing facilities by further investment, however, consideration must be given to two other means of increasing output: greater utilisation of existing capacity, by additional shift working, overtime, and so on, or the provision of new capacity at a new location, whether to supplement the existing plant or even to replace it as well. The first of these choices—increasing plant utilisation—largely involves additional operating costs, although some small capital expenditure in the area of staff facilities and maintenance areas may be required. The latter, on the other hand, will open up a whole range of possibilities and will require very careful evaluation. Fundamentally the analysis requires determining the present value of the total costs of producing on the existing plant—which will rise over time both as average costs rise and because aggregate output is increasing the longer the plant is operated—and the present value of the cost of installing the new plant and of producing on it. The second of these values will clearly fall the longer the delay in installing the new plant. Comparison of the growing value of the first item with the value of the second, which will fall by progressively smaller amounts, will indicate the point of time when the new plant should be brought into operation when the present value of the total production costs will be minimised. Similar sets of costs can also be compared to assess whether the existing plant should be retained once the new plant is brought into operation or whether the incremental cost of additional new capacity—on top of that required to *expand* output—is less than the cost of keeping the old plant in operation.

This method of evaluation will be found to be usable however complicated the relationship between total production costs and output, so that extra items of capital expenditure which cause steps to occur in the cost curve can be relatively easily handled. Detailed examples of the method are given in reference A 11.

From the purely financial standpoint, certain key areas should be examined. Can the expansion be financed in whole or in part from borrowed funds without transgressing any gearing limits of the existing business? Will further equity capital be required, and, if so, what is the current value of the company's shares? (See Chapter 11, Section 3 for a fuller discussion on this point.) Can the existing business absorb the additional tax allowances available on the new investment? Can the flow of dividends to the shareholders be maintained during the development of the expansion? Will the expansion cause disruptions to reported profits? These are all financial questions which consideration of the capital cost of the scheme should trigger.

b. Examination of major construction problems[1]

It is commonplace for companies engaged in the consideration of major construction projects to take the decision on whether or not to proceed with a project with the combined advice both of the engineers and of financial advisers. It is less common, but, in our opinion, no less desirable for the whole planning and execution of such projects similarly to be undertaken by a team which, while recognising the rightful major role of engineers, contains sufficient financial expertise on a full-time basis to permit a full financial analysis to be available at every stage and for every major component. The danger of not permitting this integrated approach is that, throughout the planning of the project which is being undertaken

[1] Reference A11.

solely by engineers, there will be a series of minor decisions taken which embody implicit or crude financial analysis. It has been shown in many large construction projects that the full-time involvement in the engineers' team of one or more expert and imaginative financial analysts can make a significant contribution not simply to reducing project costs but, more importantly, to improving the profitability on the project.

There are a number of areas in all construction projects where thorough financial analysis can be rewarding. The following discussion illustrates some of the relevant aspects:

(i) *Choice of equipment*

Right through the engineering planning and design of a project there will be a series of choices made about individual units of equipment: all too easily these choices will be made according to rules of thumb with their origins in some financial precept—such as a three year payback criterion—but with little relevance to the project under study. Yet by considering the choice of every component of a major project as a separate, though minor, project in its own right, numerous questions will be thrown up, the answers to which will enable the profitability of the whole project to be improved. For instance, should the choice be made for expensive equipment requiring little maintenance over a long life, or is a more frequent replacement policy of cheaper items to be adopted? Is it better to choose the lower cost equipment produced locally and to pay the supplier's normal terms, or to buy the more expensive imported plant financed as part of a long-term export credit? Is the plant to be designed initially for its ultimate levels of capacity, or should it be installed in modules which will permit a gradual phasing up to full capacity?

The answers to all these and other similar questions concerning sub-components of the entire project can be easily found by engineers and financial analysts working in concert; having agreed the alternatives to be considered, their capital and operating costs, lives, and so on can be estimated and the NPV's of each can be evaluated. The financial analyst will be particularly concerned to assess the availability and value of investment incentives for the investing company, bearing in mind the possibility that it might already have so great a volume of tax deductions that there is little present value in further immediate tax allowances. Operating costs should be carefully analysed and broken down into their fixed and variable elements so that the cash flows can properly reflect the impact of rising or fluctuating output. Particular attention must be paid to comparing the levels of skill required to operate different types of equipment, so that the correct choice may be made between, say, the lowest cost package of sub-units forming a total plant demanding skilled labour and supervision, or the dearer but integrated system which minimises operating skills and costs.

This discussion should indicate that it is not necessarily correct, in the interests of total project profitability, to choose always the least cost components, or those offering the fastest payback or the lowest interest rates; nor is it enough for the analyst to assess the entire project as an investment decision. Close co-operation between financial and engineering disciplines throughout the planning phases of a project can be of tremendous value. One further consideration reinforcing this is that often some of the engineers and of the financial analysts will 'grow up' with the project and become part of its operating staff; not only will their involvement in the design stage stand them in good stead, but also, conversely, their anticipation of operational problems will greatly assist their analysis of design questions.

(ii) *Installation of excess capacity*

In a typical production process consisting of several discrete units of plant, the possibility of installing every unit to the same optimum level of capacity is remote; often it is further complicated by the feeling that at some stage expansion might be justified, and that the provision of excess capacity in some areas can, therefore, be justified on the grounds of this expectation, even though the increased outlets cannot be forecast with any certainty. In such cases not only is there no substitute for a thorough analysis of the financial consequences of the various choices, but furthermore such analysis frequently reveals a larger range of possibilities, some of them far more satisfactory, than those believed to exist as a result of prior judgement and in-tuition.

As a first step, the actual designed capacities at each stage of the process and the economies of scale of each main process element, should be identified and quantified. This step by itself often yields the surprising result both that the entire process has substantial excess capacity already built-in but unrealised, and that with little additional refinement the capacity could be even further expanded. In some cases the decision will be taken to reduce certain engineering provisions and bring the capacity back into line with the original requirements; in other cases what had been regarded as a market constraint may turn out to have resulted from assumptions about levels of production costs which, with improvements to total plant design, can be reduced. Instances where sensible anticipation of an increased demand would suggest the provision of excess capacity in certain key areas, such as site preparation, piling, and so on, abound, but without an inter-disciplinary approach to planning and design these advantages are less likely to be perceived.

(iii) *Construction time and procedure*

The marketing and financial requirements of the timing of construction often run counter to normal engineering standards. Frequently it will be worth incurring additional capital costs to complete construction early in order to seize a particular market opportunity, particularly if fiscal incentives and the availability of loan finance reduce the sensitivity of the investor to the capital cost of the project. On the other hand, there will be occasions when financial analysis suggests that a longer construction period than normal might be preferable: a smaller but more reliable labour force might then be used, or experiments might be made with different suppliers of plant or methods of construction.

Forecasts of cost inflation might suggest certain forms of construction procedure, such as a project labour contract, which would otherwise not be recommended by the engineer. Knowledge of the financing package, combined with the technical knowledge of the engineers, might require special forms of project insurance to be taken out. Supplies of common facilities—transport, power, materials, catering—should be examined to see whether provision by the owner, rather than by the contractor can obtain these at lower prices or less risk. These are further instances of the desirability of close involvement of financial as well as technical experts throughout the design and planning stage.

c. Leasing and lease or buy projects[1]

Most companies will be involved in leasing problems in one form or another, and for some companies leasing projects will be the most

---

[1] Reference A 8.

common of all. Every company will face the problem of whether to lease or buy its offices. Companies controlling stores or warehouses, oil companies controlling service stations, breweries controlling public houses, and shipping companies all face the problems of leasing versus purchase. While the alternative of purchasing rather than leasing assets can be looked on as a cost saving investment (the costs saved being lease payments), these leasing problems differ from normal capital projects in their often extensive financial implications.

For example, if a company decides to purchase rather than to lease, it will sometimes be the case, because of the highly marketable character of the asset involved, that the company will be able to raise an exceptionally high proportion of debt capital secured on this specific asset. On the other hand, if the leasing alternative is taken, the existence of extensive lease commitments may have serious repercussions on the company's credit status since the fixed nature of the lease obligations may be held to be a substantial impairment of the security which the company could otherwise offer to other direct lenders.

Because of the fixed and long term nature of some of the relevant net cash flows, in particular the lease payments, risk allowance is at a minimum in most lease or buy projects and so relatively small differences in DCFs or NPVs justify one course of action rather than another. Finally, the effect of inflation is probably more significant in lease or buy projects than in any others and this factor needs to be taken carefully into account.

d. Evaluating overseas projects[1]

A problem of common occurrence in international companies is that of determining how best to finance overseas subsidiaries. Once these subsidiaries are established, there arise the related problems of evaluating their earnings and deciding what to do with them. These would be relatively straightforward and would involve no more complications than would arise in the case of a local subsidiary were it not for the problems and opportunities created by differential tax rates.

The financing problem arises in deciding how best to finance an overseas project taking into account the special tax concessions commonly granted, particularly in underdeveloped countries. The problem of evaluating earnings arises because dividends remitted to a parent company will often be heavily taxed by either the overseas country or the parent company's country, or by both. This means that

[1]Reference A 13, particularly section 2.

any dividends remitted will effectively bear the full tax rate applicable to the parent company and hence the very substantial local tax advantages can be completely nullified as regards distributed profits.

Given these disadvantages of remitting profits there is a strong temptation for profits to be retained overseas even when there is little likelihood of reinvesting them profitably. This has led to two opposing views in evaluating overseas projects. One view holds that the relevant net cash flow from an overseas project should be evaluated net only of local tax as typically the funds so earned should be reinvested locally as this is likely to be the most profitable course of action. The other view is that all overseas projects should be evaluated on the basis that all profits will be remitted to the parent company as this is the ultimate destination of all profits earned overseas and this makes projects in different countries comparable both with one another and with investment opportunities in the parent company's country. Further, it is argued that it is impossible to estimate with any precision whether profits will actually have to be remitted or not and therefore it is prudent to evaluate overseas projects on the assumption that all profits will have to be remitted to the parent company as earned.

There is merit in both views and in certain circumstances one approach or the other is appropriate; but in other circumstances neither is adequate and the evaluation of the project needs to be made along the lines developed in reference A 13, section 2. It is certainly a point in favour of an overseas project if it is profitable enough to permit the full and immediate remittance of all its net earnings to the parent company even though this involves heavy tax payments. This being so every overseas project should be subject to this test because projects which can pass it are obviously very attractive. But any project failing this test should not automatically be rejected, especially if its earnings have a strong likelihood of being required for further and profitable reinvestment overseas. Once this possibility exists then it is no longer possible to look at a particular project on its individual merits alone. It must be considered in conjunction with the other projects its earnings will be used to finance.

References

1. EZRA SOLOMONS, *The Theory of Financial Mangement*, Columbia University Press, 1963.
2. MYRON J. GORDON, *The Investment, Financing and Valuation of the Corporation*, Richard D. Irwin Inc., 1962.

Appendix A

Basic accounting principles and terminology

1. Introduction

Many aspects of investment appraisal and financial analysis necessitate an understanding of basic accounting principles and terminology. What follows is nothing more than a brief summary of the most relevant important accounting principles and terminology commonly involved in investment appraisal.

Accounting records are designed to record systematically all the monetary transactions of a business. Whenever a cost is incurred or a sale agreed, the fact is recorded in the appropriate account. From this it follows that such documents constitute a comprehensive historical record of the transactions of a business.

Published accounting documents fall into two categories; a statement about net earnings (the profit and loss account) and a statement about wealth (i.e. assets and liabilities, known as the balance sheet), and these are published annually by all joint stock limited liability companies. Their contents are as follows:

2. Profit and loss account

This account shows the net earnings[1] arising during a year, and how

[1] By 'net earnings' is meant the income arising from running the business rather than any increase in the value of the assets employed to produce that income. An example will make this clearer. Suppose a company runs a chain of supermarkets, many of them occupying prominent sites whose value is rising. Unless one of the sites were actually sold off, normal accounting practice would ignore this increasing value. Hence, the profit and loss account would contain only the net profit from running the supermarkets as supermarkets. If one of the sites were sold off during a year, the difference between its sale price and its value as recorded in the accounts would not be recorded in the profit and loss account as it is a 'capital' as distinct from a 'trading' profit. Further, it would not usually be regarded as available for distribution as a dividend.

they are divided up between the debenture holders and any other suppliers of long term loans, the different classes of shareholders, and the tax authorities. It begins with a statement of operating or trading profit before tax, followed by the deduction of (i), interest on all forms of loan capital, and (ii), *accounting* (as opposed to *tax allowable*) depreciation. Since in many countries tax payments during a year are based on profits earned in the previous year, the tax liability shown in the profit and loss account does not always correspond to the tax payment made during the year. Hence, the current net cash flow cannot always be derived simply from the current annual profit and loss statement. After deducting the tax liability, we have net profit after company tax. From this are deducted any preference share dividends, which leaves net profits available to the ordinary or equity shareholders. Any interim dividend or proposed final dividend is subtracted, leaving the balance of profits to be retained in the business.

The profit and loss account will also state the balance of retained profits from previous years which are also available for payment of dividends. Hence, in any year the dividend payment can exceed the profits earned for the ordinary shareholders by drawing on past retained profits.

The profit and loss account shows the increase in 'wealth' during the accounting period, but not the form it takes. This is shown in the balance sheet. It will be apparent that profits earned will not necessarily take the form of cash; they can have been used for investment in other assets, or to reduce liabilities such as debts.

3. Balance sheet

A balance sheet is a statement of a company's wealth, and of the aggregate claims on that wealth by those lending funds to the company, such as creditors, banks, debenture holders, etc., and residually by those investing in the company, the preference and equity shareholders. It is in two halves, known respectively as the statements of assets and of liabilities. All the assets are due to some claimant, hence, the two sides of the balance sheet will, by definition, be equal. After the claims of all third parties have been satisfied—tax authorities, creditors, debenture holders, etc.—the residue belongs to the shareholders of the company. The prior claim on this residue is held by the preference shareholders (if any) in proportion to the paid up value of their shares. The balance, if any, belongs entirely to the ordinary shareholders.

The various items which go to make up a balance sheet are comprised in the following main categories:

ASSETS

(i) *Intangible assets*

For example, goodwill, trademarks, licensing agreements, patents, etc., usually at original cost less any subsequent write-offs.

(ii) *Fixed assets*

Land, buildings, plant, machinery, tools, vehicles, furniture, fitments, etc.—usually shown at original cost (occasionally at a revaluation) less total depreciation written off to date.

(iii) *Trade investments*

Usually investments in subsidiary or associated companies, both equity and loan, usually shown at cost at the time of acquisition plus net loans made since, and hence often revealing little information.

(iv) *Current assets*

Assets which will normally be turned into cash within a year—even where the cash is normally reinvested in the same assets, e.g. stocks, trade debtors and cash. Also included are quoted investments (i.e. investments quoted on a stock exchange), and payments in advance, e.g. on account of rent, etc.

LIABILITIES

(i) *Share capital*, etc.

Ordinary shares—at par (i.e. nominal) value.[1]

Preference shares—at par (i.e. nominal) value.[1]

[1] This assumes that the shares are fully paid up, i.e. that cash or equivalent assets are deemed to have been paid into the company to the full value of the shares. Shares are not always issued fully paid. It is possible to issue a share with, say, a 50p nominal value on which only 25p has to be paid at the time of issue, the remaining 25p being available to be called at some future date. Such shares are said to be only 'partly paid up'. Where such shares exist only the value paid up is shown in the balance sheet. Partly paid up shares occur most commonly in new companies which prefer to receive their initial equity funds in instalments. They are very rare in established companies as they constitute an unwelcome contingent liability for the equity shareholders. Should such a company go into liquidation (of its own choice or otherwise) with insufficient resources to pay off all creditors, lenders and preference shareholders in full, then the equity shareholders are liable to pay up the balance outstanding on the partly paid shares.

Capital reserves—reserves arising from 'capital' profits, such as issuing shares at a premium, or from capital gains.

Revenue reserves—i.e. retained profits (distributable as dividends).

(ii) *Long term liabilities*

Loans, debentures, etc.

(iii) *Current liabilities (i.e. liabilities which fall due within a year)*

Bank overdrafts and other short-term loans, tax payments, trade creditors, prospective dividend and interest payments.

(iv) *Contingent liabilities*

These comprise such items as legally contracted obligations to pay money in certain cases, e.g. capital expenditure; also such items as potential damages in a law suit. It should be noted that 'contingent liabilities' do not form part of the total liabilities but appear in the form of a note to the balance sheet. In short, they comprise supplementary information.

The total value of the 'assets' will, of course, equal the total value of the 'liabilities'.

The balance sheet usually shows asset values at cost of acquisition less any depreciation written off in the case of fixed assets, and sometimes of intangible assets also. Stocks are valued at original (historic) cost, or market value, whichever is lower, but accounting principles permit a choice in the way these costs are computed. The main variants are FIFO, LIFO, and average cost.

FIFO is the abbreviation for 'first in first out'. This is the traditional method which assumes that items are withdrawn from stock in the strict order in which they were put in; i.e. the oldest item of stock is always assumed to be withdrawn first. LIFO or 'last in first out', is the opposite of FIFO, and under this method the newest item of stock is assumed to be consumed first. Average cost or AVCO is, as its name implies, an average of all past costs.

Whichever variant is being used, when a business is being valued for the purpose of purchase, stocks should be valued on a current basis. This will normally be at replacement cost, assuming the continuation of the business. Where the business is not to be continued, resale value is the appropriate valuation.

Clearly, none of the values comprising a balance sheet, save perhaps the cash balance, need be worth the sums stated. For this reason the balance sheet is merely a starting point for the ascertainment of current values.

4. The relationship between the balance sheet and the profit and loss account

The balance sheet is a statement of the wealth of a business at a given time. The profit and loss account records the changes in wealth during a given period due to the interaction of costs and revenues. Hence, it helps to explain the changes between balance sheets. It will not explain all the changes in wealth as some of these are of a capital nature. For instance, if the business raises more capital, or uses its cash to buy machines or repay debts, none of these items affects the costs or revenues of the business, hence, they would not appear in the profit and loss account, but would show up only in the balance sheet. Because of the rules governing the drawing up of the balance sheet, all these transactions will have a twofold effect so that both the assets and liabilities remain in equilibrium. If the business raises more capital, then the liabilities side of the balance sheet will increase, and will be counterbalanced by an exactly similar increase of cash on the assets side. When cash is used to buy machines, then the amount of cash will fall by exactly the amount by which the value of the total fixed assets will increase, i.e. the two changes both happen on the same side of the balance sheet and cancel out. When cash is used to repay creditors, then both assets and liabilities are reduced by the same amount.

As an example of changes which affect the profit and loss account also, suppose an asset costing £1,000 is being depreciated by 10% in a given year. The £100 of depreciation appears in the profit and loss account as a cost, and reduces profits accordingly. In the balance sheet the value of fixed assets is reduced by £100 and profits, as we have seen, have been reduced equally so that the balance sheet remains in equilibrium. Similarly, when wages are paid, cash (an asset) is reduced and so are profits (a liability). The relation between the two accounting documents is thus simple and direct.

5. The effect of balance sheet statements on debt capital

Certain balance sheet ratios are important in financial appraisals, notably long term debt to net tangible assets. Net tangible assets are usually defined to mean total tangible assets less current liabilities. It is usually the case that the amount of long-term debt capital a business can raise is restricted to a certain proportion of its net tangible assets, often around 25%–30%, although the actual amount varies from industry to industry, and country to country.

It is clear that where such rules are being applied, the way in which accounts are drawn up can affect the total borrowing open to a company. Where fixed assets are written down as fast as possible, however laudable this may be on some grounds, it is to the detriment of a company's ability to raise money as cheaply as possible. Similarly, where there has been marked inflation and fixed assets are shown only on the written down historic cost basis, a wide gap exists between this value and the current value of the assets in question. To the extent that the assets are not written up to reflect their current value, the scope for borrowing cheaply is necessarily reduced.

References

1. H. C. EDEY, *Introduction to Accounting*, Hutchinson, 1963.
2. H. C. EDEY, *Business Budgets and Accounts*, Hutchinson, 1960.

Appendix B

Definitions: cash flows, working capital, etc.[1]

The logic underlying all the discounting methods determines the precise net cash flow data to be used in their applications. This section considers more fully the definitions of net cash flows given in Chapter 1 of '. . . profits less taxes when paid plus the depreciation provisions'.

1. General definitions

Net cash flows are the *incremental* cash receipts less the incremental expenditures solely attributable to the decision to proceed with an investment. Cash expenditures typically comprise the capital outlays necessary to commence a project (including working capital) and to replace capital items during its life. They can also comprise operating losses. Cash receipts typically comprise profits and depreciation provisions net of actual tax payments at the time they occur. They also include the recovery of capital (e.g. the residual or scrap value of assets) and working capital at the end of a project's life. With the typical average delay of eighteen months between the earning of taxable profits and the payment of taxes thereon, there is an important distinction between tax payments and the *accounting* provision for taxes made in the same years as taxable profits are earned.

2. Depreciation provision

The inclusion of depreciation provisions as part of the net cash flows of a project may at first seem incorrect. But all the discounting methods automatically allow fully for the recovery of capital from the net cash flows, hence it is correct to include the accounting depreciation provisions as a part of the net cash flows. This has the important

[1] Reference A 2, Section 2.

advantage that the discounting profitability assessment is not affected by the pattern of accounting depreciation chosen.

3. Interest payments

It should also be noted that because of the following treatment and definition of net working capital, the net cash flows should be net of interest payments on the debt used to finance working capital.

4. Net working capital

Net working capital for *investment appraisal purposes* is defined as follows:

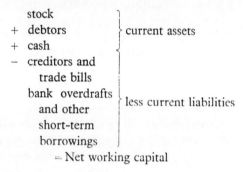

$$
\begin{array}{l}
\ \text{stock} \\
+\ \text{debtors} \\
+\ \text{cash} \\
-\ \text{creditors and} \\
\ \ \text{trade bills} \\
\ \ \text{bank overdrafts} \\
\ \ \text{and other} \\
\ \ \text{short-term} \\
\ \ \text{borrowings} \\
=\ \text{Net working capital}
\end{array}
$$

current assets

less current liabilities

In this definition current liabilities differ from those so defined for normal accounting purposes. The latter normally include dividends and tax payments due to be paid within a year (see Appendix A for a brief explanation of accounting principles and terminology). Both these items have been excluded in the above definition of current liabilities and hence of working capital. Tax payments are excluded because they are deducted from profits in computing the net cash flows, and to treat them also as a source of finance would be double counting the benefit from delayed tax payments. Dividends due are excluded as a source of finance because they form a *share* of the net cash flow earned by a company and cannot therefore be treated also as a source of the finance for the project to which they relate. Net working capital thus defined is the net sum which has to be financed from *long-term* capital, that is shareholders' funds plus long-term debt. The net working capital required for a project is thus just a part of the capital outlay. It is convenient to treat the *initial* net working capital requirement as part of the capital outlays, but any subsequent requirements (resulting from increased output) should be deducted from the project's earnings in computing the annual net cash flows since money tied up in net working capital is not available for other uses outside the project. Similarly, any net working capital recovered when output falls or when the project terminates should be treated as additions to the annual net cash flows.

5. Net residual asset values, etc.

During, or more commonly, at the end of a project's life, it will often be possible to recover some value from the residual assets, either through resale, or employing them usefully elsewhere within the organisation. Such residual values, net of handling charges, etc. and tax charges (or allowances) should be added to the net cash flows. The same applies to any miscellaneous receipts associated with a project which fall into none of the previously mentioned categories.

Appendix C

Some short-cut methods for evaluating tax burdens and investment incentives

I. Derivation of general tax formulae

The derivation of the *general* present value formulae for the various types of tax allowable depreciation of investment allowance (other than outright grants) is as follows. In particular cases such as the regime in the U.K. in 1972/3 when no investment allowances (tax allowable depreciation in excess of 100% of the asset value) were available this variable would be set at zero.

Consider the present value P of the following tax allowances that arise in the case of the reducing balance method of tax depreciations allowances, assuming tax relief to arise at yearly intervals from the purchase of the asset, discounted at the rate r.

Years: 0   1   2   3

$$P = tC(V+R+d) + \frac{tdCm}{(1+r)} + \frac{tdCm(1-d)}{(1+r)^2} + \frac{tdCm(1-d)^2}{(1+r)^3} + \cdots$$

$$+ \frac{tdCm(1-d)^{n-1}}{(1+r)^n} + \frac{t(W-S)}{(1+r)^n}$$

where C = initial capital cost,
      n = life of the asset in years,
      t = percentage rate of tax,
      d = percentage rate of depreciation on the reducing balance method,
      V = percentage investment allowance,

R = percentage initial allowance,
S = the lower of the resale value at end-year n, and C,
W = written down value at end-year n, and
$m = (1 - R - d)$.

This series arises in the following manner. Each £1 of depreciation saves a firm tax at rate t. In the first year (assumed initially to be at the start of the first year, that is, the time of purchase of the asset) the firm is allowed as an expense for tax purposes $(V + R + d)\%$ of the capital cost C. Thus the tax saved is $tC(V + R + d)$. The written down value of the asset for tax purposes is then the initial cost C, less the initial and annual allowance only, i.e. $C(1 - R - d) = Cm$. At the end of the first year, the firm is allowed for its annual tax depreciation the proportion d of the written down value Cm. Hence, the tax saving is $tdCm$. Since the allowance of proportion d has been received, the written-down value for the end of the second year becomes $Cm(1 - d)$, and at the end of the third year $Cm(1 - d)^2$, to $Cm(1 - d)^{n-1}$ at the end of the nth year.

The series can be rewritten as:

$$P = tC\left\{(V + R + d) + \frac{dm}{(1-d)}\left[\frac{(1-d)}{(1+r)} + \frac{(1-d)^2}{(1+r)^2} + \cdots + \frac{(1-d)^n}{(1+r)^n}\right]\right\}$$
$$+ \frac{t(W - S)}{(1+r)^n}$$

If we now put $1/(1+k) = (1-d)/(1+r)$, so that $k = (r+d)/(1-d)$, the formula reduces to

$$P = tC\left[(V + R + d) + \frac{dm}{(1-d)}(a_{n|k})\right] + \frac{t(W-S)}{(1+r)^n}$$

The balancing allowance, or charge, $(W - S)$, is the difference between S (the lower initial cost and resale value) and the written down value of C for tax purposes at the end of the nth year, that is $W = Cm(1 - d)^n$. Thus the present value of the balancing allowance, or charge, can be rewritten as

$$\frac{t[Cm(1-d)^{n-1} - S]}{(1+r)^n} = \frac{tCm(1-d)^n}{(1+r)^n} - \frac{tS}{(1+r)^n}$$
$$= \frac{tCm}{(1+k)^n} - \frac{tS}{(1+r)^n}$$

If this expression is substituted for $t(W-S)/(1+r)^n$ in the full series, and allowance is made for the fact that the average delay between capital expenditure and receipt of tax relief from capital allowances is assumed to be q years, then the series can assume the final form of:

$$P = \frac{tC}{(1+r)^q}\left\{(V+R+d) + \frac{dm}{(1-d)}\left[a_{n|k} + \frac{(1-d)}{d}v_{n|k}\right] - \frac{S}{C(1+r)^n}\right\}$$

To simplify the tax accounting, companies have tended to elect to continue depreciating assets for tax purposes even where the assets have in fact been disposed of. Under these circumstances the formula reduces to

$$P = \frac{tC}{(1+r)^q}\left\{(V+R+d) + \frac{dm}{(1-d)k}\right\}$$

The derivation of the formula for straight line depreciation follows much the same lines to give a present value of tax savings (including the balancing allowance at end-year n) of

$$P = \frac{tC}{(1+r)^q}\left\{(V+R+d) + da_{n|r} + \left[(1-R-nd) - \frac{S}{C}\right]v_{n|r}\right\}$$

Using these general formulae, the values of capital allowances and grants and of after-tax revenues and costs can be calculated. Appendix Table C which follows contains a wide range of percentage value factors which can be used as 'ready reckoners' in evaluations undertaken under the 1972/3 U.K. tax rules and, with slight modification, in many other instances.

Tables

A   The present value of £1

B   The present value of £1 per annum

C   Percentage present values of capital allowances and grants, and of net-of-tax revenues and costs

Appendix Table A

Appendix Table A The Present Value of 1

Year	1	2	3	4	5	6	7	8	9	10
					Percentage					
1	0·990099	0·980392	0·970874	0·961538	0·952381	0·943396	0·934579	0·925926	0·917431	0·909091
2	0·980296	0·961169	0·942596	0·924556	0·907029	0·889996	0·873439	0·857339	0·841680	0·826446
3	0·970590	0·942322	0·915142	0·888996	0·863838	0·839619	0·816298	0·793832	0·772183	0·751315
4	0·960980	0·923845	0·888487	0·854804	0·822702	0·792094	0·762895	0·735030	0·708425	0·683013
5	0·951466	0·905731	0·862609	0·821927	0·783526	0·747258	0·712986	0·680583	0·649931	0·620921
6	0·942045	0·887971	0·837484	0·790315	0·746215	0·704961	0·666342	0·630170	0·596267	0·564474
7	0·932718	0·870560	0·813092	0·759918	0·710681	0·665057	0·622750	0·583490	0·547034	0·513158
8	0·923483	0·853490	0·789409	0·730690	0·676839	0·627412	0·582009	0·540269	0·501866	0·466507
9	0·914340	0·836755	0·766417	0·702587	0·644609	0·591898	0·543934	0·500249	0·460428	0·424098
10	0·905287	0·820348	0·744094	0·675564	0·613913	0·558395	0·508349	0·463193	0·422411	0·385543
11	0·896324	0·804263	0·722421	0·649581	0·584679	0·526788	0·475093	0·428883	0·387533	0·350494
12	0·887449	0·788493	0·701380	0·624597	0·556837	0·496969	0·444012	0·397114	0·355535	0·318631
13	0·878563	0·773033	0·680951	0·600574	0·530321	0·458839	0·414964	0·367698	0·326179	0·289664
14	0·859963	0·757875	0·661118	0·577475	0·505068	0·442301	0·387817	0·340461	0·299246	0·263331
15	0·861349	0·743015	0·641852	0·555265	0·481017	0·417265	0·352446	0·315242	0·274538	0·239392
16	0·852821	0·728446	0·623167	0·533908	0·458112	0·393646	0·338735	0·291890	0·251870	0·217629
17	0·844377	0·714163	0·605016	0·513373	0·435297	0·371364	0·316574	0·270269	0·231073	0·197845
18	0·836017	0·700159	0·587395	0·493628	0·415521	0·350344	0·295864	0·250249	0·211994	0·179859
19	0·827740	0·686431	0·570286	0·474642	0·395734	0·330513	0·276508	0·231712	0·194490	0·163508
20	0·819544	0·672971	0·553676	0·456387	0·376889	0·311805	0·258419	0·214548	0·178431	0·148644
21	0·811430	0·659776	0·537549	0·438834	0·358942	0·294155	0·241513	0·198656	0·163698	0·135131
22	0·803396	0·646839	0·521893	0·421955	0·341850	0·277505	0·225713	0·183941	0·150182	0·122846

Appendix Table A

23	0·795442	0·634156	0·506692	0·405726	0·325571	0·261797	0·210947	0·170315	0·137781	0·111678
24	0·787556	0·621721	0·491934	0·390121	0·310068	0·246979	0·197147	0·157699	0·126405	0·101526
25	0·779768	0·609531	0·477606	0·375117	0·295303	0·232599	0·184249	0·146018	0·115968	0·092296
26	0·772048	0·597579	0·463695	0·360689	0·281241	0·219810	0·172195	0·135202	0·106393	0·083905
27	0·764404	0·585862	0·450189	0·346817	0·267848	0·207368	0·160930	0·125187	0·097608	0·076278
28	0·756836	0·574375	0·437077	0·333477	0·255094	0·195630	0·150402	0·115914	0·089548	0·069343
29	0·749342	0·563112	0·424346	0·320651	0·242946	0·184557	0·140563	0·107328	0·082155	0·063039
30	0·741923	0·552071	0·411987	0·308319	0·231377	0·174110	0·131367	0·099377	0·075371	0·057309
31	0·734577	0·541246	0·399987	0·296460	0·220359	0·164255	0·122773	0·092016	0·069148	0·052099
32	0·727304	0·530633	0·388337	0·285058	0·209866	0·154957	0·114741	0·085200	0·063438	0·047362
33	0·720103	0·520229	0·377026	0·274094	0·199873	0·146186	0·107235	0·078889	0·058200	0·043057
34	0·712973	0·510028	0·366045	0·263552	0·190355	0·137912	0·100219	0·073045	0·053395	0·039143
35	0·705914	0·500028	0·355383	0·253415	0·181290	0·130105	0·093663	0·067635	0·048986	0·035584
36	0·698925	0·490223	0·345032	0·243669	0·172657	0·122741	0·087535	0·062625	0·044941	0·032349
37	0·692005	0·480611	0·334983	0·234297	0·164436	0·115793	0·081809	0·057986	0·041231	0·029408
38	0·685153	0·471187	0·325226	0·225285	0·156605	0·109239	0·076457	0·053650	0·037826	0·026735
39	0·678370	0·461948	0·315754	0·216621	0·149148	0·103056	0·071455	0·049713	0·034703	0·024304
40	0·671653	0·452890	0·306557	0·208289	0·142046	0·097222	0·066780	0·046031	0·031838	0·022095
41	0·665003	0·444010	0·297628	0·200278	0·135282	0·091719	0·062412	0·042261	0·029209	0·020086
42	0·658419	0·435304	0·288959	0·192575	0·128840	0·086527	0·058329	0·039464	0·026797	0·018260
43	0·651900	0·426769	0·280543	0·185168	0·122704	0·081630	0·054513	0·036541	0·024584	0·016600
44	0·645445	0·418401	0·272372	0·178046	0·116861	0·077009	0·050946	0·033834	0·022555	0·015091
45	0·639055	0·410197	0·264439	0·171198	0·111297	0·072650	0·047613	0·031328	0·020692	0·013719
46	0·632728	0·402154	0·256737	0·164614	0·105997	0·068538	0·044499	0·029007	0·018984	0·012472
47	0·626463	0·394268	0·249259	0·158283	0·100949	0·064658	0·041587	0·026859	0·017416	0·011338
48	0·620260	0·386538	0·241999	0·152195	0·096142	0·060998	0·038867	0·024869	0·015978	0·010307
49	0·614119	0·378958	0·234950	0·146341	0·091564	0·057546	0·036324	0·023027	0·014659	0·009370
50	0·608039	0·371528	0·228107	0·140713	0·087204	0·054288	0·033948	0·021321	0·013449	0·008519

Appendix Table A

Appendix Table A The present value of 1

Year	11	12	13	14	15	16	17	18	19	20
1	0.900901	0.892857	0.884956	0.877193	0.869565	0.862069	0.854701	0.847458	0.840336	0.833333
2	0.811622	0.797194	0.783147	0.769468	0.756144	0.743163	0.730514	0.718184	0.706165	0.694444
3	0.731191	0.711780	0.693050	0.674972	0.657516	0.640658	0.624371	0.608631	0.593416	0.578704
4	0.658731	0.635518	0.613319	0.592080	0.571753	0.552291	0.533650	0.515789	0.498669	0.482253
5	0.593451	0.567427	0.542760	0.519369	0.497177	0.476113	0.456111	0.437109	0.419049	0.401878
6	0.534541	0.505631	0.480319	0.455587	0.432328	0.410442	0.389839	0.370432	0.352142	0.334898
7	0.481658	0.452349	0.425061	0.399637	0.375937	0.353830	0.333195	0.313925	0.295918	0.279082
8	0.433926	0.403883	0.376160	0.350559	0.326902	0.305025	0.284782	0.266038	0.248671	0.232568
9	0.390325	0.350610	0.332885	0.307508	0.284262	0.262953	0.243404	0.225456	0.208967	0.193807
10	0.352184	0.321973	0.294588	0.269744	0.247185	0.226684	0.208037	0.191064	0.175602	0.161506
11	0.317283	0.287476	0.260698	0.236617	0.214943	0.195417	0.177810	0.161919	0.147565	0.134588
12	0.285841	0.256675	0.230706	0.207559	0.186907	0.168463	0.151974	0.137220	0.124004	0.112157
13	0.257514	0.229174	0.204165	0.182069	0.162528	0.145227	0.129892	0.116288	0.104205	0.093464
14	0.231995	0.204620	0.180677	0.159710	0.141329	0.125195	0.111019	0.098549	0.087567	0.077887
15	0.209004	0.182696	0.159891	0.140096	0.122894	0.107927	0.094888	0.083316	0.073586	0.064905
16	0.188292	0.163122	0.141496	0.122892	0.106865	0.093041	0.081101	0.070776	0.061837	0.054088
17	0.169633	0.145644	0.125218	0.107300	0.092926	0.080207	0.069317	0.059980	0.051964	0.045073
18	0.152822	0.130040	0.110812	0.094561	0.080805	0.069144	0.059245	0.050830	0.043667	0.037561
19	0.137678	0.116107	0.098034	0.082948	0.070265	0.059607	0.050637	0.043077	0.036695	0.031301
20	0.124034	0.103567	0.086782	0.072762	0.061100	0.051385	0.043280	0.036506	0.030836	0.026084
21	0.111742	0.092560	0.076798	0.063826	0.053131	0.044298	0.036991	0.030937	0.025913	0.021737
22	0.100669	0.082643	0.067963	0.055988	0.046201	0.038188	0.031616	0.026218	0.021775	0.018114

Percentage

Appendix Table A

23	0·090693	0·073788	0·060144	0·049112	0·040174	0·032920	0·027022	0·022218	0·018299	0·015095
24	0·081705	0·065882	0·053225	0·043081	0·034934	0·028380	0·023096	0·018829	0·015377	0·012579
25	0·073608	0·058823	0·047102	0·037790	0·030378	0·024465	0·019740	0·015957	0·012922	0·010483
26	0·066314	0·052521	0·041683	0·033149	0·026415	0·021091	0·016872	0·013523	0·010859	0·008735
27	0·059742	0·046894	0·036888	0·029078	0·022970	0·018182	0·014421	0·011460	0·009125	0·007280
28	0·053822	0·041859	0·032544	0·025507	0·019974	0·015674	0·012325	0·009712	0·007668	0·006066
29	0·048488	0·037383	0·028889	0·022375	0·017369	0·013512	0·010534	0·008230	0·006444	0·005055
30	0·043683	0·033378	0·025565	0·019627	0·015103	0·011648	0·009004	0·006975	0·005415	0·004213
31	0·039354	0·029802	0·022624	0·017217	0·013133	0·010042	0·007696	0·005911	0·004550	0·003511
32	0·035454	0·026609	0·020021	0·015102	0·011420	0·008657	0·006577	0·005009	0·003824	0·002926
33	0·031940	0·023758	0·017718	0·013248	0·009931	0·007463	0·005622	0·004245	0·003213	0·002438
34	0·028775	0·021212	0·015680	0·011621	0·008635	0·006433	0·004805	0·003598	0·002700	0·002032
35	0·025924	0·018940	0·013876	0·010194	0·007509	0·005546	0·004107	0·003049	0·002269	0·001693
36	0·023355	0·016910	0·012279	0·008942	0·006529	0·004781	0·003510	0·002584	0·001907	0·001411
37	0·021040	0·015098	0·010867	0·007844	0·005678	0·004121	0·003000	0·002190	0·001602	0·001176
38	0·018955	0·013481	0·009617	0·006880	0·004937	0·003553	0·002564	0·001856	0·001347	0·000980
39	0·017077	0·012036	0·008510	0·006035	0·004293	0·003063	0·002192	0·001573	0·001132	0·000816
40	0·015384	0·010747	0·007531	0·005294	0·003733	0·002640	0·001873	0·001333	0·000951	0·000680
41	0·013850	0·009595	0·006665	0·004644	0·003246	0·002276	0·001601	0·001129	0·000799	0·000576
42	0·012486	0·008567	0·005898	0·004074	0·002823	0·001962	0·001368	0·000957	0·000671	0·000472
43	0·011249	0·007649	0·005219	0·003573	0·002455	0·001692	0·001170	0·000811	0·000564	0·000394
44	0·010134	0·006830	0·004619	0·003135	0·002134	0·001458	0·001000	0·000687	0·000474	0·000328
45	0·009130	0·006098	0·004088	0·002750	0·001856	0·001257	0·000854	0·000583	0·000398	0·000273
46	0·008225	0·005445	0·003617	0·002412	0·001614	0·001084	0·000730	0·000494	0·000335	0·000228
47	0·007410	0·004861	0·003201	0·002116	0·001403	0·000934	0·000624	0·000418	0·000281	0·000190
48	0·006676	0·004340	0·002833	0·001856	0·001220	0·000805	0·000533	0·000355	0·000236	0·000158
49	0·006014	0·003875	0·002507	0·001628	0·001061	0·000694	0·000456	0·000300	0·000199	0·000132
50	0·005418	0·003460	0·002219	0·001428	0·000923	0·000599	0·000390	0·000255	0·000167	0·000110

Appendix Table A

Appendix Table A   The present value of 1

Year	\	\	\	\	Percentage	\	\	\	\	\
	21	22	23	24	25	26	27	28	29	30
1	0.825446	0.819672	0.813008	0.806452	0.800000	0.793651	0.787402	0.781250	0.775194	0.769231
2	0.683013	0.671862	0.660982	0.650334	0.640000	0.629882	0.620001	0.610352	0.600925	0.591716
3	0.554474	0.550704	0.537384	0.524487	0.512000	0.499906	0.488190	0.476837	0.465834	0.455166
4	0.455507	0.451399	0.436897	0.422974	0.409600	0.396751	0.384402	0.372529	0.361111	0.350128
5	0.385543	0.369999	0.355201	0.341108	0.327680	0.314882	0.302678	0.291038	0.279931	0.269329
6	0.318631	0.303278	0.288781	0.275087	0.262144	0.249906	0.238329	0.227374	0.217001	0.207176
7	0.263331	0.248589	0.234782	0.221844	0.209715	0.198338	0.187661	0.177636	0.168218	0.159366
8	0.217629	0.203761	0.190879	0.178907	0.167772	0.157411	0.147765	0.138778	0.130401	0.122589
9	0.179859	0.167017	0.155187	0.144280	0.134218	0.124930	0.116350	0.108420	0.101086	0.094300
10	0.148644	0.136899	0.126168	0.116354	0.107374	0.099150	0.091614	0.084703	0.078362	0.072538
11	0.122846	0.112213	0.102576	0.093834	0.085899	0.078691	0.072137	0.066174	0.060745	0.055799
12	0.101526	0.091978	0.083395	0.075673	0.068719	0.062453	0.056801	0.051699	0.047089	0.042922
13	0.083905	0.075391	0.067801	0.061026	0.054976	0.049566	0.044725	0.040390	0.036503	0.033017
14	0.069343	0.061796	0.055122	0.049215	0.043980	0.039338	0.035217	0.031554	0.028297	0.025398
15	0.057309	0.050653	0.044815	0.039689	0.035184	0.031221	0.027730	0.024652	0.021936	0.019537
16	0.047362	0.041519	0.036435	0.032008	0.028147	0.024778	0.021834	0.019259	0.017005	0.015028
17	0.039143	0.034032	0.029622	0.025813	0.022518	0.019665	0.017192	0.015046	0.013182	0.011560
18	0.032349	0.027895	0.024083	0.020817	0.018014	0.015607	0.013537	0.011755	0.010218	0.008892
19	0.026735	0.022865	0.019580	0.016788	0.014412	0.012387	0.010659	0.009184	0.007921	0.006840
20	0.022095	0.018741	0.015918	0.013538	0.011529	0.009831	0.008393	0.007175	0.006141	0.005262
21	0.018260	0.015362	0.012942	0.010918	0.009223	0.007802	0.006609	0.005605	0.004760	0.004048
22	0.015091	0.012592	0.010522	0.008805	0.007379	0.006192	0.005204	0.004379	0.003690	0.003113
23	0.012472	0.010321	0.008554	0.007101	0.005903	0.004914	0.004097	0.003421	0.002860	0.002395

Appendix Table A

24	0·010307	0·008460	0·006955	0·005726	0·004722	0·003900	0·003226	0·002673	0·002217	0·001842
25	0·008519	0·006934	0·005654	0·004618	0·003778	0·003096	0·002540	0·002088	0·001719	0·001417
26	0·007040	0·005684	0·004597	0·003724	0·003022	0·002457	0·002000	0·001631	0·001333	0·001090
27	0·005818	0·004659	0·003737	0·003003	0·002418	0·001950	0·001575	0·001274	0·001033	0·000839
28	0·004809	0·003819	0·003038	0·002422	0·001934	0·001547	0·001240	0·000996	0·000801	0·000645
29	0·003974	0·003130	0·002470	0·001953	0·001547	0·001228	0·000977	0·000778	0·000621	0·000496
30	0·003284	0·002566	0·002008	0·001575	0·001238	0·000975	0·000769	0·000608	0·000481	0·000382
31	0·002714	0·002103	0·001633	0·001270	0·000990	0·000774	0·000605	0·000475	0·000373	0·000294
32	0·002243	0·001724	0·001328	0·001024	0·000792	0·000614	0·000477	0·000371	0·000289	0·000226
33	0·001854	0·001413	0·001079	0·000826	0·000634	0·000487	0·000375	0·000290	0·000224	0·000174
34	0·001532	0·001158	0·000877	0·000666	0·000507	0·000387	0·000296	0·000226	0·000174	0·000134
35	0·001266	0·000949	0·000713	0·000537	0·000406	0·000307	0·000233	0·000177	0·000135	0·000103
36	0·001046	0·000778	0·000580	0·000433	0·000325	0·000244	0·000183	0·000138	0·000104	0·791 4*
37	0·000865	0·000638	0·000472	0·000349	0·000260	0·000193	0·000144	0·000108	0·809 4*	0·608 4
38	0·000715	0·000523	0·000385	0·000282	0·000208	0·000153	0·000114	0·843 4*	0·627 4	0·468 4
39	0·000591	0·000429	0·000312	0·000227	0·000166	0·000122	0·895 4*	0·659 4	0·486 4	0·360 4
40	0·000488	0·000351	0·000253	0·000183	0·000133	0·966 4*	0·704 4	0·515 4	0·377 4	0·277 4
41	0·000403	0·000288	0·000206	0·000148	0·000106	0·767 4	0·555 4	0·402 4	0·292 4	0·213 4
42	0·000333	0·000236	0·000167	0·000119	0·851 4*	0·609 4	0·437 4	0·314 4	0·227 4	0·164 4
43	0·000276	0·000193	0·000136	0·961 4*	0·681 4	0·483 4	0·344 4	0·245 4	0·176 4	0·126 4
44	0·000228	0·000159	0·000111	0·775 4	0·544 4	0·383 4	0·271 4	0·192 4	0·136 4	0·969 5
45	0·000183	0·000130	0·900 4*	0·625 4	0·436 4	0·304 4	0·213 4	0·150 4	0·106 4	0·746 5
46	0·000156	0·000107	0·732 4	0·504 4	0·348 4	0·242 4	0·168 4	0·117 4	0·818 5	0·574 5
47	0·000129	0·873 4*	0·595 4	0·407 4	0·279 4	0·192 4	0·132 4	0·914 5	0·634 5	0·441 5
48	0·000106	0·716 4	0·484 4	0·328 4	0·223 4	0·152 4	0·104 4	0·714 5	0·492 5	0·339 5
49	0·878 4*	0·587 4	0·393 4	0·264 4	0·178 4	0·121 4	0·820 5	0·558 5	0·381 5	0·261 5
50	0·726 4	0·481 4	0·320 4	0·213 4	0·143 4	0·958 5	0·645 5	0·436 5	0·295 5	0·201 5

* The final digit is the power of 10 by which the given tabular value has to be divided.

Appendix Table A

Appendix Table A   The present value of 1

Year	31	32	33	34	35	36	37	38	39	40
					Percentage					
1	0.763359	0.757576	0.751880	0.746269	0.740741	0.735294	0.729927	0.724638	0.719424	0.714286
2	0.582717	0.573921	0.565323	0.556917	0.548697	0.540657	0.532793	0.525100	0.517572	0.510204
3	0.444822	0.434789	0.425055	0.415610	0.406442	0.397542	0.388900	0.380507	0.372354	0.364431
4	0.339559	0.329385	0.319590	0.310156	0.301068	0.292310	0.283869	0.275730	0.267880	0.260308
5	0.259205	0.249534	0.240293	0.231460	0.223014	0.214934	0.207204	0.199804	0.192720	0.185934
6	0.197866	0.189041	0.180672	0.172731	0.165195	0.158040	0.151243	0.144786	0.138647	0.132810
7	0.151043	0.143213	0.135843	0.128904	0.122367	0.116206	0.110397	0.104917	0.099746	0.094865
8	0.115300	0.108495	0.102138	0.096197	0.090642	0.085445	0.080582	0.076027	0.071760	0.067760
9	0.088015	0.082193	0.076795	0.071789	0.067142	0.062828	0.058819	0.055092	0.051626	0.048400
10	0.067187	0.062267	0.057741	0.053574	0.049735	0.046197	0.042933	0.039922	0.037141	0.034572
11	0.051288	0.047172	0.043414	0.039980	0.036841	0.033968	0.031336	0.028929	0.026720	0.024694
12	0.039151	0.035737	0.032642	0.029836	0.027289	0.024977	0.022875	0.020963	0.019223	0.017639
13	0.029886	0.027073	0.024543	0.022266	0.020214	0.018365	0.016697	0.015190	0.013830	0.012599
14	0.022814	0.020510	0.018453	0.016616	0.014974	0.013504	0.012187	0.011008	0.009949	0.008999
15	0.017415	0.015538	0.013875	0.012400	0.011092	0.009929	0.008896	0.007977	0.007158	0.006428
16	0.013294	0.011771	0.010432	0.009254	0.008216	0.007301	0.006493	0.005780	0.005149	0.004591
17	0.010148	0.008918	0.007844	0.006906	0.006086	0.005368	0.004740	0.004188	0.003705	0.003280
18	0.007747	0.006756	0.005898	0.005154	0.004508	0.003947	0.003460	0.003035	0.002665	0.002343
19	0.005914	0.005118	0.004434	0.003846	0.003339	0.002902	0.002525	0.002199	0.001917	0.001673
20	0.004514	0.003877	0.003334	0.002870	0.002474	0.002134	0.001843	0.001594	0.001379	0.001195
21	0.003446	0.002937	0.002507	0.002142	0.001832	0.001569	0.001345	0.001155	0.000992	0.000854
22	0.002630	0.002225	0.001885	0.001598	0.001357	0.001154	0.000982	0.000837	0.000714	0.000610
23	0.002008	0.001686	0.001417	0.001193	0.001005	0.000848	0.000717	0.000606	0.000514	0.000436

Appendix Table A

	C1	C2	C3	C4	C5	C6	C7	C8	C9	C10
24	0·001533	0·001277	0·001066	0·000890	0·000745	0·000624	0·000523	0·000439	0·000370	0·000311
25	0·001170	0·000968	0·000801	0·000664	0·000552	0·000459	0·000382	0·000318	0·000266	0·000222
26	0·000893	0·000733	0·000602	0·000496	0·000409	0·000337	0·000279	0·000231	0·000191	0·000159
27	0·000682	0·000555	0·000453	0·000370	0·000303	0·000248	0·000203	0·000167	0·000138	0·000113
28	0·000520	0·000421	0·000341	0·000276	0·000224	0·000182	0·000149	0·000121	0·990 4*	0·810 4*
29	0·000397	0·000319	0·000256	0·000204	0·000166	0·000134	0·000108	0·878 4*	0·712 4	0·578 4
30	0·000303	0·000241	0·000193	0·000154	0·000123	0·986 4*	0·791 4*	0·636 4	0·512 4	0·413 4
31	0·000232	0·000183	0·000145	0·000115	0·911 4*	0·725 4	0·578 4	0·461 4	0·369 4	0·295 4
32	0·000177	0·000139	0·000109	0·856 4*	0·675 4	0·533 4	0·422 4	0·334 4	0·265 4	0·211 4
33	0·000135	0·000105	0·818 4*	0·639 4	0·500 4	0·392 4	0·308 4	0·242 4	0·191 4	0·151 4
34	0·000103	0·795 4*	0·615 4	0·477 4	0·370 4	0·288 4	0·225 4	0·175 4	0·137 4	0·108 4
35	0·786 4*	0·602 4	0·463 4	0·356 4	0·274 4	0·212 4	0·164 4	0·127 4	0·987 5	0·768 5
36	0·600 4	0·456 4	0·348 4	0·266 4	0·203 4	0·156 4	0·120 4	0·921 5	0·710 5	0·549 5
37	0·458 4	0·346 4	0·262 4	0·198 4	0·151 4	0·115 4	0·874 5	0·558 5	0·511 5	0·392 5
38	0·350 4	0·262 4	0·197 4	0·148 4	0·112 4	0·842 5	0·638 5	0·484 5	0·368 5	0·280 5
39	0·267 4	0·198 4	0·148 4	0·110 4	0·826 5	0·619 5	0·465 5	0·351 5	0·264 5	0·200 5
40	0·204 4	0·150 4	0·111 4	0·824 5	0·612 5	0·455 5	0·340 5	0·254 5	0·190 5	0·143 5
41	0·156 4	0·114 4	0·836 5	0·615 5	0·453 5	0·335 5	0·248 5	0·184 5	0·137 5	0·102 5
42	0·119 4	0·863 5	0·628 5	0·459 5	0·336 5	0·246 5	0·181 5	0·133 5	0·985 6	0·729 6
43	0·906 5	0·654 5	0·472 5	0·342 5	0·249 5	0·181 5	0·132 5	0·966 6	0·709 6	0·521 6
44	0·692 5	0·495 5	0·355 5	0·255 5	0·184 5	0·133 5	0·964 6	0·700 6	0·510 6	0·372 6
45	0·528 5	0·375 5	0·267 5	0·191 5	0·136 5	0·979 6	0·704 6	0·508 6	0·367 6	0·266 6
46	0·403 5	0·284 5	0·201 5	0·142 5	0·101 5	0·720 6	0·514 6	0·358 6	0·264 6	0·190 6
47	0·308 5	0·215 5	0·151 5	0·106 5	0·749 6	0·529 6	0·375 6	0·266 6	0·190 6	0·136 6
48	0·235 5	0·163 5	0·114 5	0·792 6	0·555 6	0·389 6	0·274 6	0·193 6	0·137 6	0·968 7
49	0·179 5	0·124 5	0·854 6	0·591 6	0·411 6	0·286 6	0·200 6	0·140 6	0·982 7	0·691 7
50	0·137 5	0·936 6	0·642 6	0·441 6	0·304 6	0·210 6	0·146 6	0·101 6	0·707 7	0·494 7

* The final digit is the power of 10 by which the given tabular value has to be divided.

Appendix Table B

Appendix Table B The present value of 1 per annum

Year	\multicolumn{10}{c}{Percentage}									
	1	2	3	4	5	6	7	8	9	10
1	0·990099	0·980392	0·970874	0·961538	0·952381	0·943396	0·934579	0·925926	0·917431	0·909091
2	1·97040	1·94156	1·91347	1·88609	1·85941	1·63339	1·80802	1·73326	1·75911	1·73554
3	2·94099	2·88388	2·82861	2·77509	2·72325	2·67301	2·62432	2·57710	2·53129	2·48685
4	3·90197	3·80773	3·71710	3·62990	3·54595	3·46511	3·38721	3·31213	3·23972	3·16987
5	4·85343	4·71346	4·57971	4·45182	4·32948	4·21236	4·10020	3·99271	3·88965	3·79079
6	5·79548	5·60143	5·41719	5·24214	5·07569	4·91732	4·76654	4·62288	4·48592	4·35526
7	6·72819	6·47199	6·23028	6·00205	5·78637	5·58238	5·38929	5·20637	5·03295	4·86842
8	7·65168	7·32548	7·01969	6·73274	6·46321	6·20979	5·97130	5·74664	5·53482	5·33493
9	8·56602	8·16224	7·78611	7·43533	7·10782	6·80169	6·51523	6·24689	5·99525	5·75902
10	9·47130	8·98259	8·53020	8·11090	7·72173	7·36009	7·02358	6·71008	6·41766	6·14457
11	10·3676	9·78685	9·25262	8·76048	8·30641	7·88687	7·49867	7·13896	6·80519	6·49506
12	11·2551	10·5753	9·95400	9·38507	8·86325	8·38384	7·94269	7·53608	7·16073	6·81369
13	12·1337	11·3484	10·6350	9·98565	9·39357	8·85268	8·35765	7·90378	7·48690	7·10336
14	13·0037	12·1062	11·2961	10·5631	9·89864	9·29498	8·74547	8·24424	7·78615	7·36669
15	13·8651	12·8493	11·9379	11·1184	10·3797	9·71225	9·10791	8·55948	8·06069	7·60608
16	14·7179	13·5777	12·5611	11·6523	10·8378	10·1059	9·44665	8·85137	8·31256	7·82371
17	15·5623	14·2919	13·1661	12·1657	11·2741	10·4773	9·76322	9·12164	8·54363	8·02155
18	16·3983	14·9920	13·7535	12·6593	11·6896	10·8276	10·0591	9·37189	8·75563	8·20141
19	17·2260	15·6785	14·3238	13·1339	12·0853	11·1581	10·3356	9·60360	8·95011	8·36492
20	18·0456	16·3514	14·8775	13·5903	12·4622	11·4699	10·5940	9·81815	9·12855	8·51356
21	18·8570	17·0112	15·4150	14·0292	12·8212	11·7641	10·8355	10·0168	9·29224	8·64869
22	19·6604	17·6580	15·9369	14·4511	13·1630	12·0416	11·0612	10·2007	9·44243	8·77154

Appendix Table B

23	20.4558	18.2922	16.4436	14.8558	13.4886	12.3034	11.2722	10.3711	9.58021	8.88322
24	21.2434	18.9139	16.9355	15.2470	13.7986	12.5504	11.4693	10.5288	9.70661	8.98474
25	22.0232	19.5235	17.4131	15.6221	14.0939	12.7834	11.6536	10.6748	9.82258	9.07704
26	22.7952	20.1210	17.8768	15.9828	14.3752	13.0032	11.8258	10.8100	9.92897	9.16095
27	23.5596	20.7069	18.3270	16.3296	14.6430	13.2105	11.9867	10.9352	10.0266	9.23722
28	24.3164	21.2813	18.7641	16.6631	14.8981	13.4062	12.1371	11.0511	10.1161	9.30657
29	25.0658	21.8444	19.1885	16.9837	15.1411	13.5907	12.2777	11.1584	10.1983	9.36961
30	25.8077	22.3965	19.6004	17.2920	15.3725	13.7648	12.4090	11.2578	10.2737	9.42691
31	26.5423	22.9377	20.0004	17.5885	15.5928	13.9291	12.5318	11.3498	10.3428	9.47901
32	27.2696	23.4683	20.3888	17.8736	15.8027	14.0840	12.6466	11.4350	10.4062	9.52638
33	27.9897	23.9886	20.7658	18.1476	16.0025	14.2302	12.7538	11.5139	10.4644	9.56943
34	28.7027	24.4986	21.1318	18.4112	16.1929	14.3631	12.8540	11.5869	10.5178	9.60857
35	29.4086	24.9986	21.4872	18.6646	16.3742	14.4982	12.9477	11.6546	10.5668	9.64416
36	30.1075	25.4888	21.8323	18.9083	16.5469	14.6210	13.0352	11.7172	10.6118	9.67651
37	30.7995	25.9695	22.1672	19.1426	16.7113	14.7368	13.1170	11.7752	10.6530	9.70592
38	31.4847	26.4406	22.4925	19.3679	16.8679	14.8460	13.1935	11.8289	10.6908	9.73265
39	32.1630	26.9026	22.8082	19.5845	17.0170	14.9491	13.2649	11.8786	10.7255	9.75696
40	32.8347	27.3555	23.1148	19.7928	17.1591	15.0463	13.3317	11.9246	10.7574	9.77905
41	33.4997	27.7995	23.4124	19.9931	17.2944	15.1380	13.3941	11.9672	10.7866	9.79914
42	34.1581	28.2348	23.7014	20.1856	17.4232	15.2245	13.4524	12.0067	10.8134	9.81740
43	34.8100	28.6616	23.9819	20.3708	17.5459	15.3062	13.5070	12.0432	10.8380	9.83400
44	35.4555	29.0800	24.2543	20.5488	17.6628	15.3832	13.5579	12.0771	10.8605	9.84909
45	36.0945	29.4902	24.5187	20.7200	17.7741	15.4558	13.6055	12.1084	10.8812	9.86281
46	36.7272	29.8923	24.7754	20.8847	17.8801	15.5244	13.6500	12.1374	10.9002	9.87528
47	37.3537	30.2866	25.0247	21.0429	17.9810	15.5890	13.6916	12.1643	10.9176	9.88662
48	37.9740	30.6731	25.2667	21.1951	18.0772	15.6500	13.7305	12.1891	10.9336	9.89693
49	38.5881	31.0521	25.5017	21.3415	18.1687	15.7076	13.7668	12.2122	10.9482	9.90630
50	39.1961	31.4236	25.7298	21.4822	18.2559	15.7619	13.8007	12.2335	10.9617	9.91481

Appendix Table B The present value of 1 per annum

Appendix Table B

Year	Percentage									
	11	12	13	14	15	16	17	18	19	20
1	0·900901	0·892857	0·884956	0·877193	0·869565	0·862069	0·854701	0·847458	0·840336	0·833333
2	1·71252	1·69005	1·66810	1·64666	1·62571	1·60523	1·58521	1·56564	1·54650	1·52778
3	2·44371	2·40183	2·36115	2·32163	2·28323	2·24589	2·20958	2·17427	2·13992	2·10648
4	3·10245	3·03735	2·97447	2·91371	2·85498	2·79818	2·74324	2·69006	2·63859	2·58873
5	3·69590	3·60478	3·51723	3·43308	3·35216	3·27429	3·19935	3·12717	3·05763	2·99061
6	4·23054	4·11141	3·99755	3·88867	3·78448	3·68474	3·58918	3·49760	3·40978	3·32551
7	4·71220	4·56376	4·42261	4·28830	4·16042	4·03857	3·92238	3·81153	3·70570	3·60459
8	5·14612	4·96764	4·79877	4·63886	4·48732	4·34359	4·20716	4·07757	3·95437	3·83716
9	5·53705	5·32825	5·13166	4·94637	4·77158	4·60654	4·45057	4·30302	4·16333	4·03097
10	5·88923	5·65022	5·42624	5·21612	5·01877	4·83323	4·65860	4·49409	4·33893	4·19247
11	6·20652	5·93770	5·68694	5·45273	5·23371	5·02864	4·83641	4·65601	4·48650	4·32706
12	6·49236	6·19437	5·91765	5·66029	5·42062	5·19711	4·98839	4·79322	4·61050	4·43922
13	6·74987	6·42355	6·12181	5·84236	5·58315	5·34233	5·11828	4·90951	4·71471	4·53268
14	6·98187	6·62817	6·30249	6·00207	5·72448	5·46753	5·22930	5·00806	4·80228	4·61057
15	7·19087	6·81086	6·46238	6·14217	5·84737	5·57546	5·32419	5·09158	4·87586	4·67547
16	7·37916	6·97399	6·60388	6·26506	5·95423	5·66850	5·40529	5·16235	4·93770	4·72956
17	7·54879	7·11963	6·72909	6·37286	6·04716	5·74870	5·47461	5·22233	4·98966	4·77463
18	7·70162	7·24967	6·83991	6·46742	6·12797	5·81785	5·53385	5·27316	5·03333	4·81219
19	7·83929	7·36578	6·93797	6·55037	6·19823	5·87746	5·58449	5·31624	5·07003	4·84350
20	7·96333	7·46944	7·02475	6·62313	6·25933	5·92884	5·62777	5·35275	5·10086	4·86958
21	8·07507	7·56200	7·10155	6·68696	6·31246	5·97314	5·66476	5·38368	5·12677	4·89132
22	8·17574	7·64465	7·16951	6·74294	6·35866	6·01133	5·69637	5·40990	5·14855	4·90943

Appendix Table B

23	4·92453	5·16685	5·43212	5·72340	6·04425	6·39584	6·79206	7·22966	7·71843	8·26643
24	4·93710	5·18223	5·45095	5·74649	6·07263	6·43377	6·83514	7·28288	7·78432	8·34814
25	4·94759	5·19515	5·46691	5·76623	6·09709	6·46415	6·87293	7·32998	7·84314	8·42174
26	4·95632	5·20601	5·48043	5·78311	6·11818	6·49056	6·90608	7·37167	7·89566	8·48806
27	4·96360	5·21513	5·49189	5·79753	6·13636	6·51353	6·93515	7·40856	7·94255	8·54780
28	4·96967	5·22280	5·50160	5·80985	6·15204	6·53351	6·96066	7·44120	7·98442	8·60162
29	4·97472	5·22924	5·50983	5·82039	6·16555	6·55088	6·98304	7·47009	8·02181	8·65011
30	4·97894	5·23466	5·51681	5·82939	6·17720	6·56598	7·00266	7·49565	8·05518	8·69379
31	4·98245	5·23921	5·52272	5·83709	6·18724	6·57911	7·01988	7·51828	8·08499	8·73315
32	4·98537	5·24303	5·52773	5·84366	6·19590	6·59053	7·03498	7·53830	8·11159	8·76860
33	4·98781	5·24625	5·53197	5·84928	6·20336	6·60046	7·04823	7·55602	8·13535	8·80054
34	4·98984	5·24895	5·53557	5·85409	6·20979	6·60910	7·05985	7·57170	8·15656	8·82932
35	4·99154	5·25122	5·53862	5·85820	6·21534	6·61661	7·07005	7·58557	8·17550	8·85524
36	4·99295	5·25312	5·54120	5·86171	6·22012	6·62314	7·07899	7·59785	8·19241	8·87859
37	4·99411	5·25472	5·54339	5·86471	6·22424	6·62881	7·08683	7·60872	8·20751	8·89963
38	4·99510	5·25607	5·54525	5·86727	6·22779	6·63375	7·09371	7·61833	8·22099	8·91859
39	4·99592	5·25720	5·54682	5·86946	6·23086	6·63805	7·09975	7·62684	8·23303	8·93567
40	4·99660	5·25815	5·54815	5·87133	6·23350	6·64178	7·10504	7·63438	8·24378	8·95105
41	4·99717	5·25895	5·54928	5·87294	6·23577	6·64502	7·10969	7·64104	8·25337	8·96491
42	4·99764	5·25962	5·55024	5·87430	6·23774	6·64785	7·11376	7·64694	8·26194	8·97740
43	4·99803	5·26019	5·55105	5·87547	6·23943	6·65030	7·11733	7·65216	8·26959	8·98865
44	4·99836	5·26066	5·55174	5·87647	6·24089	6·65244	7·12047	7·65678	8·27642	8·99878
45	4·99863	5·26106	5·55232	5·87733	6·24214	6·65429	7·12322	7·66086	8·28252	9·00791
46	4·99886	5·26140	5·55281	5·87806	6·24323	6·65591	7·12563	7·66448	8·28796	9·01614
47	4·99905	5·26168	5·55323	5·87868	6·24416	6·65731	7·12774	7·66768	8·29282	9·02355
48	4·99921	5·26191	5·55359	5·87922	6·24497	6·65853	7·12960	7·67052	8·29716	9·03022
49	4·99934	5·26211	5·55389	5·87967	6·24566	6·65959	7·13123	7·67302	8·30104	9·03624
50	4·99945	5·26228	5·55414	5·88006	6·24626	6·66051	7·13266	7·67524	8·30450	9·04165

Appendix Table B

Appendix Table B   The present value of 1 per annum

Year	Percentage									
	21	22	23	24	25	26	27	28	29	30
1	0.826446	0.819672	0.813008	0.806452	0.800000	0.793651	0.787402	0.781250	0.775194	0.769231
2	1.50946	1.49153	1.47399	1.45682	1.44000	1.42353	1.40740	1.39160	1.37612	1.36095
3	2.07393	2.04224	2.01137	1.98130	1.95200	1.92344	1.89559	1.86844	1.84195	1.81611
4	2.54044	2.49364	2.44827	2.40428	2.36160	2.32019	2.27999	2.24097	2.20306	2.16624
5	2.92598	2.86364	2.80347	2.74538	2.68928	2.63507	2.58267	2.53201	2.48300	2.43557
6	3.24462	3.16692	3.09225	3.02047	2.95142	2.88498	2.82100	2.75938	2.70000	2.64275
7	3.50795	3.41551	3.32704	3.24232	3.16114	3.08331	3.00866	2.93702	2.86821	2.80211
8	3.72558	3.61927	3.51792	3.42122	3.32891	3.24073	3.15643	3.07579	2.99862	2.92470
9	3.90543	3.78628	3.67310	3.56550	3.46313	3.36566	3.27278	3.18421	3.09970	3.01900
10	4.05403	3.92318	3.79927	3.68186	3.57050	3.46481	3.36439	3.26892	3.17806	3.09154
11	4.17692	4.03540	3.90185	3.77569	3.65640	3.54350	3.43653	3.33509	3.23881	3.14734
12	4.27845	4.12737	3.98524	3.85136	3.72512	3.60595	3.49333	3.38679	3.28590	3.19026
13	4.36235	4.20277	4.05304	3.91239	3.78010	3.65552	3.53806	3.42718	3.32240	3.22328
14	4.43170	4.26456	4.10816	3.96160	3.82408	3.69485	3.57327	3.45873	3.35070	3.24867
15	4.48901	4.31522	4.15298	4.00129	3.85926	3.72607	3.60100	3.48339	3.37264	3.26821
16	4.53637	4.35673	4.18941	4.03330	3.88741	3.75085	3.62284	3.50265	3.37264	3.28324
17	4.57551	4.39077	4.21904	4.05911	3.90993	3.77052	3.64003	3.51769	3.40282	3.29480
18	4.60786	4.41866	4.24312	4.07993	3.92794	3.78613	3.65357	3.52945	3.41304	3.30369
19	4.63460	4.44152	4.26270	4.09672	3.94235	3.79851	3.66422	3.53863	3.42096	3.31053
20	4.65669	4.46027	4.27862	4.11026	3.95388	3.80834	3.67262	3.54580	3.42710	3.31579
21	4.67495	4.47563	4.29156	4.12117	3.96311	3.81615	3.67923	3.55141	3.43186	3.31984
22	4.69004	4.48822	4.30208	4.12998	3.97049	3.82234	3.68443	3.55579	3.43555	3.32296

Appendix Table B

n										
23	4·70251	4·49854	4·31063	4·13708	3·97639	3·82725	3·68853	3·55921	3·43841	3·32535
24	4·71282	4·50700	4·31759	4·14281	3·98111	3·83115	3·69175	3·56188	3·44063	3·32719
25	4·72134	4·51393	4·32324	4·14742	3·98489	3·83425	3·69429	3·56397	3·44235	3·32861
26	4·72838	4·51962	4·32784	4·15115	3·98791	3·83670	3·69630	3·56560	3·44368	3·32970
27	4·73420	4·52428	4·33158	4·15415	3·99033	3·83865	3·69787	3·56688	3·44471	3·33054
28	4·73901	4·52810	4·33462	4·15657	3·99226	3·84020	3·69911	3·56787	3·44551	3·33118
29	4·74298	4·53123	4·33709	4·15853	3·99381	3·84143	3·70009	3·56865	3·44614	3·33168
30	4·74627	4·53379	4·33909	4·16010	3·99505	3·84240	3·70086	3·56926	3·44662	3·33203
31	4·74898	4·53590	4·34073	4·16137	3·99604	3·84318	3·70146	3·56973	3·44699	3·33235
32	4·75122	4·53762	4·34205	4·16240	3·99683	3·84379	3·70194	3·57010	3·44728	3·33258
33	4·75308	4·53903	4·34313	4·16322	3·99746	3·84428	3·70231	3·57039	3·44750	3·33275
34	4·75461	4·54019	4·34401	4·16389	3·99797	3·84467	3·70261	3·57062	3·44768	3·33289
35	4·75588	4·54114	4·34472	4·16443	3·99838	3·84497	3·70284	3·57080	3·44781	3·33299
36	4·75692	4·54192	4·34530	4·16486	3·99870	3·84522	3·70302	3·57094	3·44792	3·33307
37	4·75779	4·54256	4·34578	4·16521	3·99896	3·84541	3·70317	3·57104	3·44800	3·33313
38	4·75850	5·54308	4·34616	4·16549	3·99917	3·84556	3·70328	3·57113	3·44806	3·33318
39	4·75909	4·54351	4·34647	4·16572	3·99934	3·84569	3·70337	3·57119	3·44811	3·33321
40	4·75958	4·54386	4·34672	4·16590	3·99947	3·84578	3·70344	3·57124	3·44815	3·33324
41	4·75998	4·54415	4·34693	4·16605	3·99957	3·84586	3·70350	3·57128	3·44818	3·33326
42	4·76032	4·54438	4·34710	4·16617	3·99966	3·84592	3·70354	3·57132	3·44820	3·33328
43	4·76059	4·54458	4·34723	4·16627	3·99973	3·84597	3·70358	3·57134	3·44822	3·33329
44	4·76082	4·54473	4·34734	4·16634	3·99978	3·84601	3·70360	3·57136	3·44823	3·33330
45	4·76101	4·54486	4·34743	4·16641	3·99983	3·84604	3·70362	3·57138	3·44824	3·33331
46	4·76116	4·54497	4·34751	4·16646	3·99986	3·84606	3·70364	3·57139	3·44825	3·33331
47	4·76129	5·54506	4·34757	4·16650	3·99989	3·84608	3·70365	3·57140	3·44825	3·33332
48	4·76140	4·54513	4·34762	4·16653	3·99991	3·84610	3·70367	3·57140	3·44826	3·33332
49	4·76149	4·54519	4·34766	4·16656	3·99993	3·84611	3·70367	3·57141	3·44826	3·33332
50	4·76156	4·54524	4·34769	4·16658	3·99994	3·84612	3·70368	3·57141	3·44827	3·33333

Appendix Table B

Appendix Table B   The present value of 1 per annum

Year	Percentage									
	31	32	33	34	35	36	37	38	39	40
1	0·763359	0·757576	0·751880	0·746269	0·740741	0·735294	0·729927	0·724638	0·719424	0·714286
2	1·34608	1·33150	1·31720	1·30319	1·28944	1·27595	1·26272	1·24974	1·23700	1·22449
3	1·79090	1·76629	1·74226	1·71880	1·69588	1·67349	1·65162	1·63024	1·60935	1·58892
4	2·13046	2·09567	2·06185	2·02895	1·99695	1·96580	1·93549	1·90597	1·87723	1·84923
5	2·38966	2·34521	2·30214	2·26041	2·21996	2·18074	2·14269	2·10578	2·06995	2·03516
6	2·58753	2·53425	2·48281	2·43314	2·38516	2·33878	2·29394	2·25056	2·20860	2·16797
7	2·73857	2·67746	2·61866	2·56205	2·50752	2·45498	2·40433	2·35548	2·30834	2·26284
8	2·85387	2·78595	2·72079	2·65824	2·59817	2·54043	2·48491	2·43151	2·38010	2·33060
9	2·94189	2·86815	2·79759	2·73003	2·66531	2·60326	2·54373	2·48660	2·43173	2·37900
10	3·00907	2·93041	2·85533	2·78361	2·71504	2·64945	2·58667	2·52652	2·46887	2·41357
11	3·06036	2·97759	2·89874	2·82359	2·75188	2·68342	2·61800	2·55545	2·49559	2·43826
12	3·09951	3·01332	2·93139	2·85342	2·77917	2·70840	2·64088	2·57641	2·51481	2·45590
13	3·12940	3·04040	2·95593	2·87569	2·79939	2·72676	2·65758	2·59160	2·52864	2·46850
14	3·15221	3·06091	2·97438	2·89231	2·81436	2·74027	2·66976	2·60261	2·53859	2·47750
15	3·16963	3·07644	2·98326	2·90471	2·82545	2·75020	2·67866	2·61059	2·54575	2·48393
16	3·18292	3·08822	2·99869	2·91396	2·83367	2·75750	2·68515	2·61637	2·55090	2·48852
17	3·19307	3·09713	3·00653	2·92037	2·83975	2·76287	2·68989	2·62056	2·55460	2·49180
18	3·20082	3·10389	3·01243	2·92602	2·84426	2·76681	2·69335	2·62359	2·55727	2·49414
19	3·20673	3·10901	3·01687	2·92936	2·84760	2·76972	2·69588	2·62579	2·55919	2·49582
20	3·21124	3·11288	3·02020	2·93273	2·85008	2·77185	2·69772	2·62738	2·56057	2·49701
21	3·21469	3·11582	3·02271	2·93488	2·85191	2·77342	2·69907	2·62854	2·56156	2·49787
22	3·21732	3·11805	3·02459	2·93648	2·85327	2·77457	2·70005	2·62938	2·56227	2·49848

163

Appendix Table B

n										
23	3·21933	3·11973	3·02601	2·93767	2·85427	2·77542	2·70077	2·62998	2·56279	2·49891
24	3·22086	3·12101	3·02707	2·93856	2·85502	2·77604	2·70129	2·63042	2·56316	2·49922
25	3·22203	3·12198	3·02788	2·93922	2·85557	2·77650	2·70167	2·63074	2·56342	2·49944
26	3·22293	3·12271	3·02848	2·93972	2·85598	2·77684	2·70195	2·63097	2·56361	2·49960
27	3·22361	3·12326	3·02893	2·94009	2·85628	2·77709	2·70215	2·63114	2·56375	2·49972
28	3·22413	3·12369	3·02927	2·94036	2·85650	2·77727	2·70230	2·63126	2·56385	2·49980
29	3·22452	3·12400	3·02953	2·94057	2·85667	2·77741	2·70241	2·63135	2·56392	2·49986
30	3·22483	3·12425	3·02972	2·94072	2·85679	2·77750	2·70249	2·63141	2·56397	2·49990
31	3·22506	3·12443	3·02986	2·94084	2·85688	2·77753	2·70255	2·63146	2·56401	2·49993
32	3·22524	3·12457	3·02997	2·94092	2·85695	2·77763	2·70259	2·63149	2·56403	2·49995
33	3·22537	3·12467	3·03006	2·94099	2·85700	2·77767	2·70262	2·63152	2·56405	2·49996
34	3·22547	3·12475	3·03012	2·94104	2·85704	2·77770	2·70264	2·63153	2·56407	2·49997
35	3·22555	3·12481	3·03016	2·94107	2·85706	2·77772	2·70266	2·63155	2·56403	2·49998
36	3·22561	3·12486	3·03020	2·94110	2·85703	2·77773	2·70267	2·63155	2·56408	2·49999
37	3·22566	3·12489	3·03022	2·94112	2·85710	2·77775	2·70268	2·63156	2·56409	2·49999
38	3·22569	3·12492	3·03024	2·94113	2·85711	2·77775	2·70269	2·63157	2·56409	2·49999
39	3·22572	3·12494	3·03026	2·94114	2·85712	2·77776	2·70269	2·63157	2·56410	2·50000
40	3·22574	3·12495	3·03027	2·94115	2·85713	2·77777	2·70269	2·63157	2·56410	2·50000
41	3·22576	3·12496	3·03028	2·94116	2·85713	2·77777	2·70270	2·63157	2·56410	2·50000
42	3·22577	3·12497	3·03028	2·94116	2·85713	2·77777	2·70270	2·63158	2·56410	2·50000
43	3·22578	3·12498	3·03029	2·94117	2·85714	2·77777	2·70270	2·63158	2·56410	2·50000
44	3·22578	3·12498	3·03029	2·94117	2·85714	2·77777	2·70270	2·63158	2·56410	2·50000
45	3·22579	3·12499	3·03029	2·94117	2·85714	2·77778	2·70270	2·63158	2·56410	2·50000
46	3·22579	3·12499	3·03030	2·94117	2·85714	2·77778	2·70270	2·63158	2·56410	2·50000
47	3·22580	3·12499	3·03030	2·94117	2·85714	2·77778	2·70270	2·63158	2·56410	2·50000
48	3·22580	3·12500	3·03030	2·94117	2·85714	2·77778	2·70270	2·63158	2·56410	2·50000
49	3·22580	3·12500	3·03030	2·94117	2·85714	2·77778	2·70270	2·63158	2·56410	2·50000
50	3·22580	3·12500	3·03030	2·94118	2·85714	2·77778	2·70270	2·63158	2·56410	2·50000

Appendix C

Note on the use of Table C

Table C permits the quick evaluation of the majority of U.K. capital investments in both the Development Areas and Non-Development Areas for any rate of corporation tax. To use the table it is merely necessary to estimate the average rate of corporation tax expected in future years (this could well be different from the current rate of corporation tax) and apply this rate to the investment grant and capital allowance factors in the table.

These factors comprise the present values in both Development and Non-Development Areas of:

(i) the tax saved on capital allowances for the most common categories of capital expenditure for the most typical tax delay period of 18 months, and of

(ii) investment grants paid after 6, 12, or 18 months.

The effective net capital cost of an asset is found by subtracting from the gross capital cost the present value of the grant (if applicable) and of the tax saved on the relevant capital allowances. The present value of any grant can be found from columns IX to XI of the table. The present value of the tax saved on capital allowances is given in columns I to VIII for a variety of cases.

An example will illustrate the use of the table. Suppose an asset is to be purchased which qualifies for a 20% grant (delayed 18 months), for a 50% initial allowance and for a 25% reducing balance annual allowance. Further, suppose that the average forecast rate of corporation tax is 40%. What is the effective net capital cost of this asset for a 10% discount rate?

From column XI the present value of a 100% grant delayed 18 months is 0·8668; therefore, for a 20% grant it is simply 20% × 0·8668 = 0·1734. The present value of the 40% tax saved on the capital allowances ˆ (column IV) is simply 0·8049 × 40% = 0·3220. The combined present values of grant and allowances is thus 0·1734 + 0·3220 = 0·4954, so the effective net capital cost of the asset is 1 − 0·4954 = 0·5046, that is 50·46% of the gross capital cost.

Table C also provides effective net of tax factors for corporation tax rates of 35, 40, 50, 55, and 60%, for the most typical tax delay period of 18 months. If such factors are required for any other rates of corporation tax with the 18-month tax delay these can easily be calculated using column X of the table which relates to the present value of a 100% grant delayed 18 months. For a 10% discount rate and a 40% corporation tax rate the calculation is as follows. The 10% factor from column X is 0·8668. Multiplying this by 40% we get 0·3467. The 40% effective net of tax factor is then simply 1·0 − 0·3467 = 0·6533. This is the same factor as shown in column XIII of Table C. By a similar method effective net of tax factors for tax delay periods of 6 or 12 months can be determined using columns IX and X. Calculation of present values of tax allowances and of net of tax factors incorporating other delay periods is relatively simple if reference is made to the algebraic section of this Appendix.

Reference

1. MCDOWELL, IAN. 'The Economical Planning Period for Engineering Works', *Operations Research*, Number 4, Volume 8, July–August 1960.

Appendix
Percentage present values of capital allowances

Rate of Discount	Capital Allowances: R = Initial
	d = Annual Reducing balance
	s = Straight line
	N = Number of years in sum-of-years' digits

r	I R=100% d= 0%	II R= 0% d=25%	III R=25% d=25%	IV R=50% d=25%	V R=40% s= 4%	VI R= 0% s=20%	VII R= 0% s=10%	VIII R=0% N=4
0%	1·0000	1·0000	1·0000	1·0000	1·0000	1·0000	1·0000	1·0000
1%	0·9852	0·9568	0·9662	0·9757	0·9459	0·9659	0·9424	0·9755
2%	0·9707	0·9168	0·9348	0·9528	0·8972	0·9334	0·8894	0·9519
3%	0·9566	0·8798	0·9054	0·9310	0·8532	0·9025	0·8405	0·9292
4%	0·9429	0·8453	0·8778	0·9104	0·8132	0·8731	0·7953	0·9073
5%	0·9294	0·8133	0·8520	0·8907	0·7770	0·8450	0·7536	0·8862
6%	0·9163	0·7833	0·8276	0·8720	0·7439	0·8183	0·7149	0·8659
7%	0·9035	0·7553	0·8047	0·8541	0·7136	0·7928	0·6790	0·8463
8%	0·8910	0·7290	0·7830	0·8370	0·6858	0·7684	0·6457	0·8274
9%	0·8787	0·7043	0·7624	0·8206	0·6603	0·7451	0·6147	0·8091
10%	0·8668	0·6810	0·7430	0·8049	0·6368	0·7229	0·5859	0·7915
11%	0·8551	0·6591	0·7245	0·7898	0·6150	0·7016	0·5590	0·7745
12%	0·8437	0·6385	0·7069	0·7753	0·5949	0·6812	0·5339	0·7580
13%	0·8325	0·6189	0·6901	0·7613	0·5762	0·6617	0·5105	0·7421
14%	0·8216	0·6004	0·6741	0·7478	0·5587	0·6431	0·4005	0·7267
15%	0·8109	0·5828	0·6588	0·7349	0·5425	0·6252	0·4680	0·7118
16%	0·8004	0·5661	0·6442	0·7223	0·5272	0·6080	0·4488	0·6974
17%	0·7902	0·5503	0·6303	0·7102	0·5130	0·5916	0·4307	0·6835
18%	0·7801	0·5352	0·6169	0·6985	0·4995	0·5758	0·4137	0·6699
19%	0·7703	0·5209	0·6040	0·6872	0·4869	0·5606	0·3977	0·6568
20%	0·7607	0·5072	0·5917	0·6762	0·4750	0·5460	0·3827	0·6442
21%	0·7513	0·4941	0·5798	0·6656	0·4638	0·5320	0·3686	0·6318
22%	0·7421	0·4816	0·5684	0·6553	0·4531	0·5185	0·3552	0·6199
23%	0·7331	0·4696	0·5574	0·6452	0·4430	0·5056	0·3426	0·6083
24%	0·7242	0·4582	0·5469	0·6355	0·4334	0·4931	0·3306	0·5971
25%	0·7155	0·4472	0·5367	0·6261	0·4243	0·4811	0·3194	0·5862
26%	0·7070	0·4367	0·5268	0·6169	0·4156	0·4695	0·3087	0·5756
27%	0·6987	0·4266	0·5173	0·6080	0·4073	0·4584	0·2985	0·5653
28%	0·6905	0·4169	0·5081	0·5993	0·3994	0·4476	0·2889	0·5553
29%	0·6825	0·4076	0·4993	0·5909	0·3918	0·4372	0·2798	0·5456
30%	0·6747	0·3987	0·4907	0·5827	0·3845	0·4272	0·2711	0·5361
31%	0·6669	0·3900	0·4823	0·5746	0·3776	0·4176	0·2629	0·5269
32%	0·6594	0·3717	0·4743	0·5668	0·3709	0·4082	0·2551	0·5180
33%	0·6520	0·3738	0·4665	0·5592	0·3644	0·3992	0·3476	0·5093
34%	0·6447	0·3660	0·4589	0·5518	0·3582	0·3905	0·2405	0·5008
35%	0·6375	0·3586	0·4516	0·5446	0·3523	0·3821	0·2337	0·4926
36%	0·6305	0·3514	0·4445	0·5375	0·3465	0·3740	0·2272	0·4845
37%	0·6236	0·3445	0·4375	0·5306	0·3410	0·3661	0·2210	0·4767
38%	0·6169	0·3378	0·4308	0·5238	0·3356	0·3585	0·2151	0·4691
39%	0·6102	0·3313	0·4243	0·5172	0·3305	0·3511	0·2904	0·4617
40%	0·6037	0·3251	0·4179	0·5108	0·3254	0·3440	0·2040	0·4544
41%	0·5973	0·3190	0·4118	0·5045	0·3206	0·3371	0·1988	0·4474
42%	0·5910	0·3131	0·4057	0·4984	0·3159	0·3304	0·1938	0·4405
43%	0·5848	0·3074	0·3999	0·4923	0·3113	0·3239	0·1890	0·4338
44%	0·5787	0·3019	0·3942	0·4864	0·3069	0·3176	0·1845	0·4272
45%	0·5727	0·2966	0·3886	0·4807	0·3026	0·3115	0·1801	0·4209
46%	0·5669	0·2914	0·3832	0·4750	0·2985	0·3056	0·1758	0·4146
47%	0·5611	0·2864	0·3779	0·4695	0·2944	0·2998	0·1718	0·4085
48%	0·5554	0·2815	0·3728	0·4641	0·2905	0·2943	0·1679	0·4026
49%	0·5498	0·2768	0·3678	0·4588	0·2866	0·2888	0·1641	0·3968
50%	0·5443	0·2722	0·3629	0·4536	0·2829	0·2836	0·1065	0·3911

These factors are based on a 100% tax rate and on a tax payment delay period of 18 months. They can be converted to give the present values of capital allowances for any desired tax rate merely by multiplying the relevant factor from this table by the chosen tax rate. For example, for a 40% tax rate, 10% discount rate and capital allowances as specified in column I the appropriate factor is 0·4610 × 0·40 = 0·1844. Further notes on the use of Table C are given on page 164. Columns IX to

Table C
and grants, and net-of-tax revenues and costs

Grants — Grants delayed for p months			Effective net-of-tax factors $1 - \dfrac{t}{(1+r)^{1\frac{1}{2}}}$						Rate of Discount
IX p = 6 months	X p = 12 months	XI p = 18 months	XII t = 35%	XIII t = 40%	XIV t = 45%	XV t = 50%	XVI t = 55%	t = 60%	
1·0000	1·0000	1·0000	0·6500	0·6000	0·5500	0·5000	0·4500	0·4000	0%
0·9950	0·9901	0·9852	0·6552	0·6059	0·5567	0·5074	0·4581	0·4089	1%
0·9901	0·9804	0·9707	0·6602	0·6117	0·5632	0·5146	0·4661	0·4176	2%
0·9853	0·9709	0·9566	0·6652	0·6173	0·5695	0·5217	0·4739	0·4260	3%
0·9806	0·9615	0·9429	0·6700	0·6229	0·5757	0·5286	0·4814	0·4343	4%
0·9759	0·9524	0·9294	0·6747	0·6282	0·5818	0·5353	0·4888	0·4423	5%
0·9713	0·9434	0·9163	0·6793	0·6335	0·5877	0·5418	0·4960	0·4502	6%
0·9667	0·9346	0·9035	0·6838	0·6386	0·5934	0·5483	0·5031	0·4579	7%
0·9623	0·9259	0·8910	0·6882	0·6436	0·5991	0·5545	0·5100	0·4654	8%
0·9578	0·9174	0·8787	0·6924	0·6485	0·6046	0·5606	0·5167	0·4728	9%
0·9535	0·9091	0·8668	0·6966	0·6533	0·6099	0·5666	0·5233	0·4799	10%
0·9492	0·9009	0·8551	0·7007	0·6580	0·6152	0·5725	0·5297	0·4869	11%
0·9449	0·8929	0·8437	0·7047	0·6625	0·6203	0·5782	0·5360	0·4938	12%
0·9407	0·8850	0·8325	0·7086	0·6670	0·6254	0·5838	0·5421	0·5005	13%
0·9366	0·8772	0·8216	0·7125	0·6714	0·6303	0·5892	0·5481	0·5071	14%
0·9325	0·8696	0·8109	0·7162	0·6757	0·6351	0·5946	0·5540	0·5135	15%
0·9285	0·8621	0·8004	0·7199	0·6798	0·6398	0·5998	0·5598	0·5198	16%
0·9245	0·8547	0·7902	0·7234	0·6839	0·6444	0·6049	0·5654	0·5259	17%
0·9206	0·8475	0·7801	0·7269	0·6879	0·6489	0·6099	0·5709	0·5319	18%
0·9167	0·8403	0·7703	0·7304	0·6919	0·6533	0·6148	0·5763	0·5378	19%
0·9129	0·8333	0·7607	0·7337	0·6957	0·6577	0·6196	0·5816	0·5436	20%
0·9091	0·8264	0·7513	0·7370	0·6995	0·6619	0·6243	0·5868	0·5492	21%
0·9054	0·8197	0·7421	0·7403	0·7032	0·6661	0·6290	0·5918	0·5547	22%
0·9017	0·8130	0·7331	0·7434	0·7068	0·6701	0·6335	0·5968	0·5602	23%
0·8980	0·8065	0·7242	0·7465	0·7103	0·6741	0·6379	0·6017	0·5655	24%
0·8944	0·8000	0·7155	0·7496	0·7138	0·6780	0·6422	0·6065	0·5707	25%
0·8909	0·7937	0·7070	0·7525	0·7172	0·6818	0·6465	0·6111	0·5758	26%
0·8874	0·7874	0·6987	0·7555	0·7205	0·6856	0·6506	0·6157	0·5808	27%
0·8839	0·7812	0·6905	0·7583	0·7238	0·6893	0·6547	0·6202	0·5857	28%
0·8805	0·7752	0·6825	0·7611	0·7270	0·6929	0·6587	0·6246	0·5905	29%
0·8771	0·7692	0·6747	0·7639	0·7301	0·6964	0·6627	0·6289	0·5952	30%
0·8737	0·7634	0·6669	0·7666	0·7332	0·6999	0·6665	0·6332	0·5998	31%
0·8704	0·7576	0·6594	0·7692	0·7362	0·7033	0·6703	0·6373	0·6044	32%
0·8671	0·7519	0·6520	0·7718	0·7392	0·7066	0·6740	0·6414	0·6088	33%
0·8639	0·7463	0·6447	0·7744	0·7421	0·7099	0·6777	0·6454	0·6132	34%
0·8607	0·7407	0·6375	0·7769	0·7450	0·7131	0·6812	0·6494	0·6175	35%
0·8575	0·7353	0·6305	0·7793	0·7478	0·7163	0·6847	0·6532	0·6217	36%
0·8544	0·7299	0·6236	0·7817	0·7506	0·7194	0·6882	0·6570	0·6258	37%
0·8513	0·7246	0·6169	0·7841	0·7533	0·7224	0·6916	0·6607	0·6299	38%
0·8482	0·7194	0·6102	0·7864	0·7559	0·7254	0·6949	0·6644	0·6339	39%
0·8452	0·7143	0·6037	0·7887	0·7585	0·7283	0·6982	0·6680	0·6378	40%
0·8422	0·7092	0·5973	0·7901	0·7611	0·7312	0·7014	0·6715	0·6416	41%
0·8392	0·7042	0·5910	0·7932	0·7636	0·7341	0·7045	0·6750	0·6454	42%
0·8362	0·6993	0·5848	0·7953	0·7661	0·7368	0·7076	0·6784	0·6491	43%
0·8333	0·6944	0·5787	0·7975	0·7685	0·7396	0·7106	0·6817	0·6528	44%
0·8305	0·6897	0·5727	0·7995	0·7709	0·7423	0·7136	0·6850	0·6564	45%
0·8276	0·6849	0·5669	0·8016	0·7733	0·7449	0·7166	0·6882	0·6599	46%
0·8248	0·6803	0·5611	0·8036	0·7756	0·7475	0·7195	0·6914	0·6634	47%
0·8220	0·6757	0·5554	0·8056	0·7778	0·7501	0·7223	0·6945	0·6668	48%
0·8192	0·6711	0·5498	0·8076	0·7801	0·7526	0·7251	0·6976	0·6701	49%
0·8165	0·6667	0·5443	0·8095	0·7823	0·7551	0·7278	0·7006	0·6734	50%

XI give the present values of a 100% grant, the receipt of which is delayed for 6, 12, or 18 months. To find the present value of any lesser grant it is merely necessary to multiply the relevant factor by the appropriate percentage grant. For example, a 20% grant which is subject to a 12 months' delay at a 10% discount rate is worth 0·9091 × 0·20 = 0·18182 in present value terms. Further notes on the use of Table C are given on page 164.

Original table devised by Margaret Walton.

Index